THE
LAST AND FIRST
ESKIMOS

Tununak, July 1977

THE LAST AND FIRST ESKIMOS

by Robert Coles

Photographs by Alex Harris

NEW YORK GRAPHIC SOCIETY · BOSTON

The photographer wishes to express his gratitude to the
Rockefeller Foundation Humanities Fellowship Program
for its support of his work in Alaska.

First edition

T 10/78

Chapter I, "The Madness of Dark," first appeared in
The American Poetry Review.

Library of Congress Cataloging in Publication Data
Coles, Robert.
  The last and first Eskimos.

  1. Eskimos — Alaska. 2. Eskimos — Alaska —
Pictorial works. I. Harris, Alex, 1949–
II. Title.
E99.E7C64   970′.004′97   78-7065
ISBN 0-8212-0737-7

Designed by Ann Lampton Curtis

New York Graphic Society books are published by
Little, Brown and Company.
Published simultaneously in Canada by
Little, Brown and Company (Canada) Limited

Printed in the United States of America

To the Eskimo people of Alaska — and especially those we have come to know in various villages along the coast and inland.

Contents

Foreword

In 1973 Alex Harris, my oldest son, Bob, and I spent some days in Alaska for the first time. We went from Fairbanks to Kotzebue, crossing the Arctic Circle in late August. A bush pilot took us up the Kobuk River to Noorvik, a community I would come to know fairly well over the years. Later, my son and I visited Nome, before returning to the United States. We left Alex Harris behind — it was the beginning, for him, of a continuing interest in and commitment to Alaska's Eskimo people. Since then he and I have kept going back to Alaska — in his case, to the villages of Shungnak and Kobuk, both considerably past Noorvik, up the Kobuk River; to the village of Selawik at the mouth of the Kugaruk River; and along the southern Bering Sea, to the coastal village of Tununak, to Nelson Island, as well as, not far away, to the settlement of Newtok. My own travels took me to Barrow, to Point Hope, to smaller coastal communities such as Kivalina and Naokok. We pursued common objectives, though one of us is a photographer, the other a child psychiatrist.

This is not the first time we have worked together — or for that matter, become sidetracked, it might be said, in the course of a particular study. In the introduction to *The Old Ones of New Mexico,* also a joint effort by Alex Harris and me, I explained how it had come about that one of our original intentions, to document visually and with words the ways Spanish-speaking children of the Southwest grow up and come to see the world, gave way for a while to what was a prior necessity, as well as (for us) a privilege and opportunity. The "old ones" up the hills of northern New Mexico had a kind of moral custody of their grandchildren. If we were to spend time with those boys and girls, and stand a fair chance of getting on with them, we had to have the sanction of their mothers' and fathers' parents. And soon enough we were quite absorbed in the daily activities of those elderly people, who taught us rather a lot about how a younger generation managed, not to mention a few things about "life" in general.

In Alaska, a somewhat similar development took place, though it was not strictly a matter of obtaining generational approval for our work. It rather soon became evident to both of us that if we were to understand the Eskimo children we had already met and hoped to meet, we would have to pay attention to a central theme in the contemporary Eskimo village life of Alaska — the accelerating change from a somewhat self-sufficient, if precarious, culture of hunting and fishing, to the world of welfare checks, food stamps, snowmobiles, motorboats, and oil pipelines that now predominates in even the more remote Eskimo settlements. It is not simply a matter of social or economic change. The world rarely stands still, and there are always generational differences, if not outright tensions. But the Eskimo children I have talked with are quite aware that they are witness to a significant change indeed, one an outsider must understand if he is to understand them — even as the Spanish-speaking children I met in northern New Mexico let me know, in their own ways, that I had to come to terms with "the old ones" if I was to have some sense of how a boy or girl grows up in that part of the Southwest.

I have tried to describe how the Eskimo children I met in Alaska grow up — what world view they come to possess as their very own. But the children kept persuading me that I ought connect their lives to something dramatic and important taking place right before everyone's eyes. And, in fact, the title of this book was supplied us by a particular child, a girl of ten who tried hard one morning (during a blizzard that kept me a houseguest of her parents for several days longer than I'd planned) to let me know what I ought to do — as she put it — "besides talking with the kids in the village." She had in mind for Alex Harris and me a somewhat broader look — at a decisive moment of Eskimo social history. In the fourth volume of *Children of Crisis* (*Eskimos, Chicanos, Indians*), I wanted to convey how her thoughts go — her hopes, worries, plans, interests. In this book, Alex Harris and I have tried to heed the following instructions — which for me amounted to a second blizzard that day: "We're not just Eskimos anymore. That's what my grandmother told me. At first I didn't know what she meant, but now I do. She meant what she said! She said that in this family we have Alaska's last and its first Eskimos. She was lying down, and I thought she was going to fall asleep after she told me that, but she didn't. She sat up, all of a sudden. She said that she was one of 'the last.' She said I'm one of 'the first.' She said I'd be lucky if I even remember when I'm older what it used to be like in our village. She said she's the child and I'm the grown-up, only she won't live long enough for me to teach her what I know.

"I thought she was talking in her sleep. I didn't understand her at all! But she helped me out. She put her head down on the bed again. She stared at the ceiling, and started describing what she did when she was my age. Then she told me what my mother did at my age — the same thing her mother did. But it's different for me, I know. I learned in school from the teachers how planes fly. They told us! I told my grandmother, and my mother. They laughed. They said that's for me to know. I've never seen a whale. I don't like fish. My mother says I'm the first Eskimo she's met who doesn't like fish. I told her she may be the last one in our family to like it so much! We were only kidding."

Not quite; they were reminding themselves of the ironies and ambiguities that accompany a significant historical moment — the passing of one way of life, the arrival of another. Side by side, within one family, the girl and her mother and her grandmother (and her brothers and her father and her grandfather) struggled to make sense of what was, is, happening — and why. And no doubt about it, as the reader will see, when old assumptions are disappearing and new ones are becoming consolidated in the minds of a people, more *why's* than usual get asked. Not only by children, either; many parents and grandparents are as curious and confused, as anxious to know and as perplexed at what is told them as their offspring. No wonder the grandmother just mentioned considered herself a hopeless innocent, and deferred, strangely, to her granddaughter. A year after that blizzard, when I again had occasion to visit the family (this time, during the all-too-brief summer), I tried to explain what I was doing with the many lessons I had learned in the various villages, settlements, communities of Alaska I visited. At the mention of a "book," I heard a sigh from the old lady: "You should write two — one about the last of my people, and one about the Eskimos just now being born." She was not, of course, being literal-minded. She had no mania for books. Nor did she really want me to divide my responses chronologically, because she hastened to add this: "We're all together here. We are all wondering what will come next."

Minds like mine, as a matter of fact, are the ones that get categorical, separate people by age, by "stage of development," and so on. She wanted to add a second book to my schedule because she was worried that I was separating the Eskimo children I knew from their elders and from a moment of death, of cultural transition, which those boys and girls were witness to, even as they were part of a birth: a different social order rapidly developing. As the fourth volume of *Children of Crisis* became longer and longer, I began to realize that there would have to be another book if the Eskimo grandmothers and parents were to have their way — that their children and grandchildren "not go to the lower forty-eight alone." What an extraordinary way of putting it! The grandmother mentioned above was referring to the book she knew I was working on: "If you are going to take our children's words to the lower forty-eight, don't forget to take ours, too. A child should not go to the lower forty-eight alone. A child is for us, today, a leader. If we lose them, we are in more trouble than ever before. Every day my grandchildren tell me things I don't know. And I remind them of what they'll soon forget! It is topsy-turvy here now."

Meanwhile, in other villages, from other Eskimos, Alex Harris was hearing roughly similar words, and finding it just as difficult to ignore one Eskimo world in favor of another — especially since they were inevitably (given the weather and the close-knit nature of family life in those settlements) so intimately connected. The result, eventually, of his consternation and mine was a determination to oblige that elderly Eskimo lday and send her words south, too. And send pictures, as well; pictures that she and others like her find so appealing — indeed, regard as almost magically revealing. One has to be with Eskimos to know how responsive they are to photographs. A people anyway attuned to the eye's field of vision as potentially lifesaving (the life of the hunter) find photographs a message of confirmation, of sanction, or (in Martin Heidegger's existentialist phrase) of "being confronted with itself." More on that later, with the help of an Eskimo or two.

Once again I want to acknowledge my close working relationship with Alex Harris, and say how much he has helped me to learn, to see, in Alaska. His "methodology" has been to go to an Eskimo settlement, come to know the various members of a family, stay with them (Eskimos are known correctly for their abiding hospitality), and try to be of some service to them. He has gone hunting and fishing; he has taught school; he has cared for children; and not least, he has shared his vision, as recorded by the camera, with dozens of boys and girls. For one of those inevitable applications in support of work by no means lavishly supported in this country, he wrote with characteristic brevity and modesty: "I do not wish to romanticize the Eskimo people with my camera, nor to take a strictly anthropological approach. I have tried — with what success, others must judge — to make a straightforward record of a living people facing up to, as best they can, serious social and economic changes. I have also, at times, been told by Eskimos that they have learned something about 'the lower forty-eight' through their friendship with me. I hope it has gone that way — back and forth."

I recall the joy and moments of intense self-recognition that this dedicated and utterly unassuming photographer brought to Eskimos, old and young alike, with that camera of his — which did not prompt self-conscious withdrawal or clever postures, but rather seemed to "go with" its owner, even as he for a while became absorbed, virtually, in the unbroken enormity of the tundra, a universe of sky and snow, touched occasionally by a fleck or two of humanity. We hope to share with others those small Arctic settlements we came to love so much, and here try to remember. We hope to reach those who live in another America, yet (how strange to remember when "up there") share a common citizenship with "them," Alaska's Eskimo people.

PHOTOGRAPHS

by Alex Harris

1. Tununak, April 1976

2. Newtok, May 1976

3. Shungnak, October 1973

4. Tununak, April 1975

5. Shungnak, April 1974

6. Newtok, May 1976

7. Tununak, April 1976

8. Newtok, May 1976

9. Tununak, May 1976

10. First Communion Day, Tununak, May 1978

11. Shungnak, September 1973

12. Newtok, May 1976

13. Newtok, July 1977

14. Playing husky, Shungnak, September 1973

15. Eskimo dancing, Tununak, April 1976

16. Friends church, Selawik, April 1974

17. Telling stories, Newtok, May 1976

18. Newtok, May 1976

19. Eskimo dancing, Tununak, April 1976

20. Newtok, May 1976

21. Caribou hunting, Ambler, October 1973

22. Seal hunting, Bering Sea at Tununak, April 1975

23. Tununak, April 1975

24. Tununak, April 1976

25. Tununak, April 1975

26. Shungnak, April 1974

27. Shungnak, October 1973

28. Tununak, April 1976

29. Tununak, May 1976

30. Haircut, Tununak, April 1976

31. Newtok, May 1976

32. (*overleaf*) Shungnak, September 1973

33. Tununak, July 1977

34. Tununak, April 1976

35. Catholic church, Tununak, April 1976

36. Deacons, Tununak, April 1976

37. Newtok, May 1976

38. Tununak, April 1976

39. Tununak, April 1976

40. After seal hunting: high tide, Tununak Bay, April 1975

41. Shungnak, April 1974

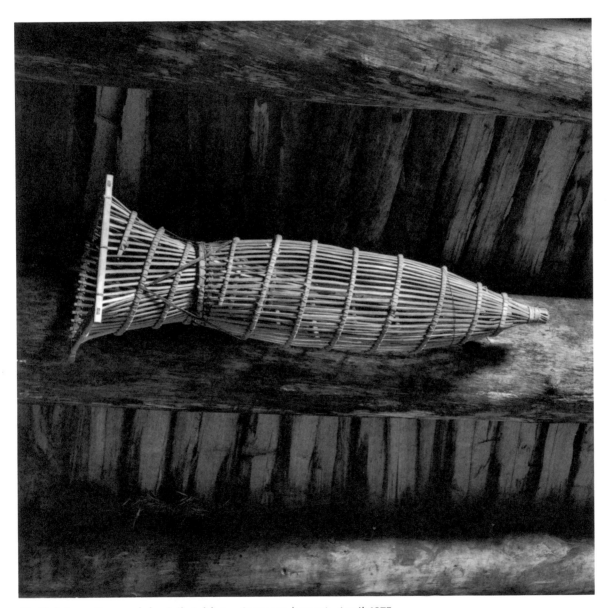

42. Fish trap, Tununak kasigik (old men's steam house), April 1975

43. Tununak, April 1976

44. Newtok, July 1977

45. Tununak, May 1976

46. Shungnak, April 1974

47. Shungnak, April 1974

48. Tundra, Newtok, May 1975

49. Abandoned sod house, Yukok, April 1975

50. Schoolhouse fire, Selawik, April 1974

51. Tununak, April 1975

52. Graveyard, Selawik, April 1974

53. Fishing, Chilugan, July 1977

54. Above the Kobuk River, Shungnak, October 1973

55. Testing the ice, Bering Sea at Tununak, April 1975

56. Shungnak, April 1974

57. Telling stories, Chilugan, July 1977

58. Newtok, May 1976

59. Newtok, May 1976

60. Shungnak, April 1974

61. Tununak, May 1976

62. Tununak, May 1976

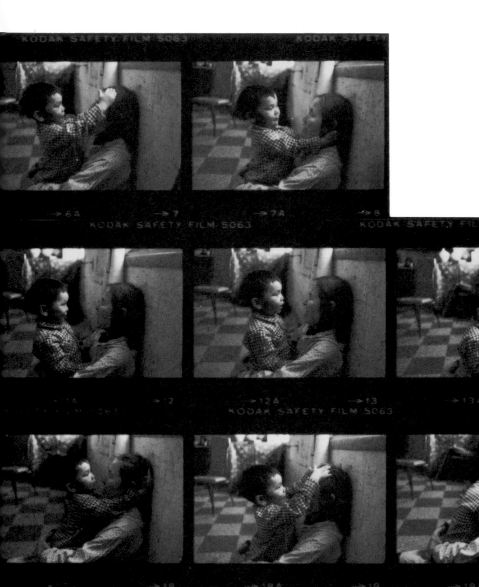

63. Newtok, July 1977

64. Newtok, July 1977

65. Newtok, July 1977

66. Newtok, July 1977

67. Willows, Shungnak, April 1974

68. Tununak, April 1976

69. Tununak, April 1976

70. Tununak, April 1976

71. Tununak Bay, twilight, April 1975

72. Friends church, Selawik, April 1974

73. Selawik, April 1974

74. Selawik, April 1974

75. Shungnak, October 1973

76. Shungnak, April 1974

77. Tununak, April 1976

78. Tununak, April 1975

THE
LAST AND FIRST
ESKIMOS

1

The Madness
of Dark

Sometimes the old Eskimo woman sits down and looks for many minutes at a rug of polar bear skin. She remembers when her husband and her brother-in-law and her young nephew brought that particular bear home. She remembers how big it was, the biggest she has ever seen, and she has seen a few in her time. She remembers how glad she was to have the skin. It is so cold, the winter floor. One can take the extremes of winter weather, but there is a "weak spot" in everyone, she insists, and for her, it has always been the feet. They make her tremble all over when they are cold. Does the visitor from the "lower forty-eight" remember what it was like when he took in an especially cold drink, or savored hard ice cream too long in his mouth? The headache that comes, the shivering in the chest, the lump of chill in the stomach — they are the body's way of saying no, stop, please be more thoughtful. Likewise, the woman's feet on a hard, frigid floor send waves of agitation up her legs, through her torso, to her head. She specifies the anatomical stages, comments on how fidgety her feet get as they pursue warmth — anywhere it is available, usually the bed — how trembling or even writhing her body gets, anxious indeed for relief from the source of marked irritation; how pointedly her eyes do their work, eventually transmitting their important message: go there, and your agony will be over.

With the polar bear skin, she has (if she remembers to use it) an island of refuge for her standing, dressing moments. It is awkward to put on stockings and socks and boots while entirely in bed; and that first step on a bare floor provides a bad jolt. Most mornings she looks at the skin before rising. Gingerly she puts the right foot on the rug, leaves the left foot dangling, reaches hard and firm for her clothes, first the footwear, which have always been placed on the skin within grabbing distance — the final thing done upon retirement each night. Then the second foot comes down, and there she is: up. In summer she can afford to be casual, forgetful; she can lose her orderly sense of what must be done and appear almost confused as she leaves the bed: where, oh where, are those clothes of mine? They may be, in July, scattered about the room. She may walk barefoot for an hour or so; and when she does get ready to go outside, the moccasins she has made herself show up at the last minute, after she has accused them of being willful, of playing games with her, of being lost. And the bearskin — she may go for days, weeks even, without paying it much attention. But in fall the rhythm of the skin and her awakening response to its presence, and her quick use of it each morning resumes, and continues for many, many months.

There is, of course, something else for the old woman to stare at, when she is of a mind to sit and look (and look and look); there is the snow. In the summer, the snow has gone — but in the summer she claims never to sit and stare. In the fall (which begins in September, and yields to winter in October, or November at the very latest) she takes up again what she once called her "position." She possesses a linguist's (and philosopher's) sense of what she has in mind: "These are the long days, the long months. The sun has its position; I have mine — the chair. I can't keep track of time, the way my children do, or my grandchildren. Even though the sun has left us, my grandson comes home from school and tells his mother what day it is. He looks at me afterward, because he knows that I will smile. I may be away from them, in the middle of my thoughts, but I know when to come back and smile. Without my smile, the boy would be disappointed. He would not be so sure of himself. To be sure of yourself, you have to see someone else smile — let you know that not everyone does things the way you do! My grandson counts the days in a month. I don't know how old I am. He thinks I am kidding him when I shrug my shoulders and say I am many winters old. He asks me, to have fun, how many. I tell him more than he would care to count up. He is sure I have done the counting. But I haven't.

"Once he asked me how many *summers* I've lived. I told him a winter or two worth of summers. He was so interested in those *numbers* they teach the children at school, he repeated his question — as if what I'd said had nothing to do with what he asked. I didn't repeat myself — and he surprised me. He *had* heard me — and understood me. He told me that he wished he could just forget all the arithmetic he was learning and play in the winters and go hunting and fishing in the summers. I told him that young people are going to have a new life. They are learning a lot, and some of them will go to the lower forty-eight and learn more. And the white men don't push our young people around the way they used to push us around. They are changing, the white people. When I sit and think of *them*, I get lost to the world. I don't hear my own daughter speaking to me."

The white people have always perplexed, if not dumbfounded, her. She has tried hard, many times, to figure them out — especially when she has been sitting in the chair. But they are no obsessions of hers. They startle her, occasionally, with their arrival in her mind; soon enough, however, she gets rid of them. It is just that, as she experiences it — a hasty housecleaning, a dismissal of sorts: "I don't like to be bothered when I'm sitting in my chair. I want to rest. I want to remember. The greatest joy for me, now, is remembering. I would be lonely if I couldn't remember. I remember my whole life. I will sit and look out the window, and suddenly I'm a young girl, and my father is holding my hand, and teaching me how to use the knife with the fish we've caught. My favorite time was with him; he would wake me up every morning, with his hand on my shoulder. I'd see his smile. He never told me to get up. My daughter tells her children to get up. We didn't talk as much then as people do now. I've caught the sickness — it's the sickness of words; no wonder I keep *saying* what I remember! I may die talking! It will serve me right!

"I will wake up, and I will see my father. He is with me. He has never left me. He will be touching my shoulder, or maybe squeezing it. He always squeezed when he was afraid I was not paying attention, or I was too much asleep. Once we went fishing, and I was moving too much. He put the line down, and he came over to me. He held my hands in his, so that they would be as still as possible. Then, just as he was going back to his line, he squeezed my shoulder. I knew what he meant. He meant that I should not forget what he'd just done — and he was afraid I would, so it's best to remind me. The other day I was going to fry some potatoes for my grandchildren, but I felt tired, and my eyes caught the large bag of potato chips. The young people of our village like potato chips more than anything else — except the Cokes they use afterwards, to wash their tongues of all the salt. I put the potatoes down, and decided not to use the stove. I picked up the bag of potato chips. But I let go of it before I really had done more than hold it in my hands. My father had seen me, and squeezed my shoulder.

"He died a long time ago. I don't know how long. Even my daughter has a number; she says thirty years — when she was a girl as old as one of my grandsons. He has a number, too. He is twelve, he tells me. So what! All these numbers. What do they have to do with life? Does the sun have numbers for itself? The bears and caribou? The fish? The snow that greets us, stays with us, goes away crying? I watch the snow cry. My grandson says it is melting. I say no, it is crying. Who likes to leave? My father died with tears in his eyes. I wiped them away, and put them to my mouth. He has been with me ever since! He used to take me to watch the snow melt. He said it was sad to see it leave, even though we were going to have a good time in the summer.

"I don't sit here and wait for the summer. I am still surprised when I hear my grandchildren say that they are counting the days until summer. Why count? Each year they talk like that. Each year I smile! I want to tell them to become more like their Eskimo ancestors, but I feel my father's squeeze on my shoulder; he always said that an Eskimo will never stop being an Eskimo, even if he goes to the lower forty-eight, and comes back here dressed up like a white man from Fairbanks. An Eskimo is born to be an Eskimo, and he may talk like the white man (my grandchildren do, more and more), but he will never stop being part of our people.

"Last winter — at the end, near melting time — I saw a man from the oil company. He came here and promised our children everything. I expected him to take the sun or the moon out of his pocket and put it on the table. I expected him to wave his pencil and turn our village into an oil well. The day may come! One of my grandchildren talks of Fairbanks; that is all I hear from her — the future she will have in the city. I feel my knees getting weak after I have listened to her. I can see her, while I sit in my chair, walking all over a big city, trying to find a home. I've never been to a big city. I don't think I would leave here without crying and crying. If the water doesn't come out of your eyes, it will go to the knees, and you will have large knees, and they will hurt a lot, and get warm. Sometimes my feet cry, even when they're not on a cold floor. On the cold floor, the feet say they hurt; when the feet cry, they are wet and sticky. I can feel that happening; I want to take my socks and my boots off. I want to go to bed and rest and think. When I think, my body stops crying — my body rests and doesn't complain about anything."

She can abruptly turn quite active and mobile. Her steps are never long, and she is, anyway, a small, slight figure; but she knows how to cross a room with all deliberate speed, and when she walks outside, she tries to cover as much territory as her energy will permit. During the winters she has a series of calls to make — touchstones of sorts to acknowledge. She will go to the shed in which the dogs sleep. She wants to look at them, say a word or two to them, and not least, feed them. It is a source of real pleasure for her to bring them meat or fish. The young Eskimos have their various offerings — including dog biscuits, for which she has utter contempt — but she will come only with meat or fish. If the dogs take the "new food" (as she describes it), that is because they have "spirits" in them that are forgetful, at least so far as food goes. Only forgetfulness, she is convinced, can explain their willingness to take things like potato chips or the soft spongy bread that comes from the store. But the dogs always remember where the river is, where the pond is, where a certain hill is. Steer them to start, and they follow their own sense of the proper destination.

She goes to the hill. She cannot, of course, always go to it in winter. But there are moments when the wind is relatively gentle, and the snow has stopped; she hitches the sled and rides with enthusiasm. The dogs bark for her, because she tells them to do so. The younger Eskimos, many of them at least, don't like to hear the dogs bark; don't even like to have much traffic with dogs. The younger Eskimos like snowmobiles, though they are no longer the rage — that was ten years ago. They are everywhere, it seems. And how *they* bark! What is the matter with the white man that he makes machines that are so noisy? The airplanes fly low and shout and bellow and make the houses tremble. The oil people have poked around, with their drills that spit and sizzle and screech. The motorboats provide an endless grating, droning sound to the summer. For her ears, however, there is only the call of the wind — and the beloved response of the dogs.

Does a visitor know that the dogs talk to the wind, having been addressed by it? The visitor seems, at best, polite. She knows how skeptical he is, but only alludes to the fact, tactfully, in the course of a story she has to tell: "Many times when I was a girl the dogs saved our lives. They could hear the wind's message before we could. By the time the wind gets us worried, it is already late; a bad storm can cover us. But the dogs hear the first wind; it whispers to the land. They don't bark loud. They move around a lot, and if they see us, they lift their heads high. Their noses are pointing in the direction of the wind. Their noses are telling the Eskimo people: it's coming from the sea — and if you know that, you'll get busy.

"I remember one time a missionary was visiting us. I was a girl, but I was almost a woman. He kept telling me I should be 'good.' I didn't know what he meant. Out of the corner of my eye I saw the dogs, pointing their noses. Their heads were very high. They weren't moving, just standing there. Then, they started to go around and around in a circle. I wanted to go get my father. He was in the village. Did he know a storm was coming? I told the missionary, finally, that we were in danger, and we'd better go get my mother, who was with my aunt, and my father. The missionary looked up at the sky. It was clear. He said that there was no storm coming. I said there was, I knew there was. He wanted to know how I knew. I told him: the dogs. He asked me to explain. I did. He laughed. He told me I was superstitious. It was the first time I heard the word, and I didn't know what he was talking about. How often I would hear that word over the years. The Eskimos were always hearing, then, that they were superstitious. But I knew what I knew! I told the missionary that I had to leave, right away. He said I wasn't being a good Eskimo; I was leaving *him!* I asked him to come along with me. He did. We reached my mother, and she joined us, and we found my father, and we went home. I remember seeing some clouds in the sky, as we came home. The dogs were beginning to howl. They were hungry, but not howling hungry. They were upset with us. Why weren't we doing something faster to protect ourselves from the storm? A dog keeps a close eye on his neighbors — people.

"Before we could do anything, the missionary had to leave; otherwise, to be polite, we would have to stand there talking with him. My father called me away to the back of our house, and said I should pretend to get sick. He told me to hold my stomach and come to him and say it hurts. I waited for him to go back to the minister, and then I came over and did what my father wanted me to do. The minister excused himself and left — after my father excused himself because he wanted to take me in the house and look after me. My mother could tell that my father and I had figured out a way to send the minister off. We watched him leaving, and suddenly the storm came upon us — like lightning in the summer. The wind pushed at us; it wanted to sweep us away. My father realized that the minister might not make it back to his church. I went with my father on the sled, to get the minister. We caught up with him, but he wanted to keep moving. He said we shouldn't worry. God would look after him. I was only a child, and I had no right to say anything. But I did. I said that the wind is God's breath, and we have to be careful, because when he blows that hard, he means for us to go inside and wait until he's decided to stop. The minister told me I was superstitious, again! Then he went on, and we went back home.

"We stayed inside for a long, long time — over a week, my grandchildren would say. It was a bad storm, but we had a good time. I helped my mother sew. We had enough food. The baby cried, but the wind was noisier than the baby. It was very hard to clear a path from the house to the shed. Later, we heard that the minister had died on his way back to the church. The storm had taken his spirit. My mother believed that the storm lasted such a long time because the minister was trying to break away from the storm; the longer his spirit fought with the wind, the worse the wind became. When the wind left us, it went to the mountains, far inland. That is where the minister's spirit is. Our ancestors are there, and I'm sure they are looking after the minister. I hope he doesn't wave his finger at them, the way he did at me when I was a girl. I can see him now, pointing at me and telling me I should listen carefully to everything he said. My grandmother told me that the white man never listens to anyone, but he expects everyone to listen to him. So, we listen! The wind isn't a good listener! The wind wants to speak, and we know how to listen. My father always told me that an Eskimo is a listener. We have survived here because we know how to listen. The white people in the lower forty-eight talk. They are like the wind; they sweep over everything. I used to think we would survive them, too. But I'm not so sure. When I look at my grandchildren, I am not sure at all!"

She worries a lot about those grandchildren. They talk so much; they expect so much. And they have received so much — too much by far, for her taste. Still, she is not a bitter, cynical woman, all too smugly self-righteous about her generation, her kind of life, as opposed to the way others live and, no doubt, will continue to live. More than anything else, she clings to the winter, ironically, as a source of hope. The Alaska winter will be the same for Eskimos, generation after generation of them. So long as there are Arctic winters, there will be Eskimos, or so she believes. Even the white people, with their pipelines and machinery and airplanes and navy stations and radar and helicopters and television sets and radio-telephones and bricks and mortar and electricity and loudspeakers and record players and (again and again she brings them up) snowmobiles; even the white people, with their motorboats and automatic rifles and telescopes and magnifying glasses and binoculars and medicines and portable X-ray machines and needles and freezers and frozen foods and cellophane bags and canned goods — even the white people bow to the winter, hide during it, run from it, acknowledge its sovereignty. There is not the slightest question in her mind that the winter is lord and master over all the acreage of "creation" she has ever seen. And it will fight to the finish, that winter, if ever seriously challenged.

She is afraid that, ultimately, the white people of "mainland" U.S.A. are headed for such a futile confrontation. She is no authority on twentieth-century technology, but she knows it is ever expanding, and she is certainly no innocent about those who wield that technology. There are moments, there are stretches of time (one had best not attempt to quantify them through even indirect questions) when she becomes at once grim, gloomy, apprehensive, agitated, and more than a little apocalyptic. She endows the visitors from the lower forty-eight states with a zeal and ambition that are themselves as potentially apocalyptic in character as her notion of what finally will take place during some (as yet distant, she hopes and believes) winter, when a struggle will be fought for the heart and soul of the Arctic.

During one winter she would eventually talk about that possibility, that coming time, that season when the dark will prevail, when a final night will be forced upon the northern people of her village and others like it: "My mind hides in the winter. My thoughts run from the world, and play all kinds of games. I don't worry. I am no missionary. I let the games be played. My body is tired, but my thoughts are full of energy. They keep a smile on my face, or they make me close my eyes, because I'm scared. I have never understood why some Eskimos drink liquor. Who needs liquor? I can get as wild as any drunken Eskimo, just by closing my eyes and letting my mind go! I say to myself: go ahead, and take this old lady, with her pains and wrinkles, someplace where she can have fun.

"For me, 'fun' is to be scared as well as to laugh. You cannot survive if you forget how to be scared. Always be ready to become scared — my father told us that over and over again. When an Eskimo forgets fear, he is ready to die. I will die, I think, in the summer, some summer when I'm sitting in the sun and have just told myself that it is warm, and it will always be warm, and life is beautiful. You hear our people say that 'life is beautiful' in the summer, but they have the wind in their ears and mountains of snow in their eyes when they say so. An Eskimo who is sitting in the sun and sees a quiet sea, and grass, grass that stretches as far as the eyes will take you, and hears the geese, the birds up here from the lower forty-eight — that Eskimo will yawn and go to sleep and the spirit will leave the body, and we will say good-bye to one of our people.''

She stops. She has a lot more to say, but she is distracted. She has become immersed in her own evocation of the moment of death. She wonders when, where — and whither. She has always hoped, secretly, that her spirit would hover over the village she has lived in all her life; but she is convinced that the wind will take the spirit to those mountains she sometimes mentions, or, perhaps, out to sea. She would not at all like that. For the sea *is* the winter, or so she says when she resumes, at another time, her talk about her mind's playful and not-so-playful exuberance: "I think I am safest when I am lying down and keeping my eyes closed, and seeing whatever the spirits of my people want to show me. They will take me all over; but when they try to pull me toward the ocean, I fight back. I am willing to stand near the shore. I love to walk along the edge of the water. But I do not want to go any further. When I start getting into the water (when I see in my mind the bottom of the ocean, or a wave coming to pull me, pull me) I fight back, I open my eyes, I get up, I take the coffeepot and heat it and drink a lot of coffee — no milk, no sugar. Coffee gives me strength to fight the sea's spirits.

"I know Eskimos who want to be near the ocean as much as possible. I prefer the river. I prefer a pond. When I was a girl I ran around a pond, around and around. I was never afraid I would fall in and drown. The ocean wants us! That's what I think sometimes when I am lying down and my eyes are closed. The waves have their hands open, ready to take you, hold you, keep you. Let the men go for seals. Let the men fight the ice floes. Let the men bring us the ocean's fish. I wish we lived nearer the mountains than the ocean. But I have always been trouble to others because of my fears. I am scared that the wind will carry me to the ocean. The water of the ocean will fill up my chest, and I will never be able to touch land again.''

Another pause; she is annoyed that she has not been sticking to the point of her remarks — an evocation of her mind's activity during the Arctic storms that batter her village for many months. She turns her back, even inside her house, on the ocean. Perhaps to let her all too hungrily observant visitor know that she is up to his tricks, as well as her own, she remarks upon what she has just done. She is as self-aware as her visitor is self-consciously on the watch. Often, visitor or no visitor, she catches herself turning her back on the Bering Sea, occasionally with a shudder. At such moments of dread, she wonders whether the final moment, that of the last breath for her aged body, has not arrived. But she has kept breathing, and she has managed to turn around. So far, so good. And when her thoughts race inland, she can be like a wonderfully optimistic child — for a while, at least: "The spirits tease each other. They hide, and wait to be found. They are shadows. It is dark. They are shadows in the dark. But there is always some light, even in the middle of the winter: the moon, the stars. The sun tries to come here in the winter, but most of the time it stops, turns around, leaves before we see it. We have time. The sun will make it to our village. We just have to wait and keep our hope high.

"Once I had a bad dream; it is a dream I often remember. We were scared that a storm would *never* end. We were told by my sister that we'd never see another summer. She was always dreaming. I fell asleep and I dreamed that the sun was covered by a black jacket. It had a zipper. Someone tried to open the zipper, but couldn't. Then it began to rain, instead of snow, and the sun was floating on the ocean, and some Eskimos were in boats trying to catch the sun, but it kept moving away. It was like a ball, bouncing on the water. The wind came hard, and blew the sun out of sight. The Eskimos were far from the shore. They stopped on some ice, and rested. Then the ice gave way; they went under. I woke up, and I went to look for the sun in the sky, as if it was summer. But it wasn't. Snow was falling, and I could hear the wind, and I was afraid. I turned to my husband; he was still breathing. My children were young then, and I could hear them breathing, too. I wasn't really awake, though. I began to believe that we had all died. I was sure that the snow and wind had carried us away. I was sure I wasn't in my own home. I wanted to get up and find out, but I was afraid to move. I looked for familiar things, but it was black dark. I pinched my arm, but I still didn't know if I was alive. My grandmother told me that some Eskimos don't die the way most Eskimos die. Some Eskimos just disappear. No one can find them. Their bones aren't anywhere. They walk into the sea, my grandmother said; or they get carried by the wind high, high toward the top of the world. They are there, but we will never get to see them. If the plane that brings us mail and food tried to fly to the top of the world, it would disappear, too. Planes have disappeared in our winters. People have disappeared. Dogs and sleds have disappeared. The missionaries say we believe in ghosts. The missionaries are ghosts, but we don't believe in them! We believe in the long winter night; it is what rules us — it and the sea."

She has decided that she has made as significantly political a remark as she is ever likely to. Best to shut up, think, stare at the small stove, sharpen a knife her daughter and son-in-law will soon be using: meat to cut up. Soon she is remembering again — past winters, so many of them. She has for a long time believed that her spirit will leave her body in the middle of a severe winter storm. She wants a little notice, so that she can celebrate. She does not like to drink much, but has on occasion enjoyed a glass of wine. It only takes that amount for her to become "lost," whereupon she leaves the house behind, moves across the tundra, toward the Brooks mountain range, or down in the direction of Anchorage or Juneau, mere names to her. She stops every once in a while — on a cloud which becomes her rug. She gazes at the earth below, wonders whether the next stop, the one after that, will yield her objective — that terrain where the sun casts its rays in the winter: "There must be some part of Alaska, or the lower forty-eight, where there is darkness *here,* and light *there.* My spirit will find the place where they meet — a storm on one side of a path, and the sun shining on the other. In between the spirits sit, facing one way, then the other. It would be a nice time for my poor spirit; it must be as tired of my body as my body is tired. I would like to take my body with me, and drop it someplace where no one would ever see it. I would like some dogs to find it, during a storm. Their owners have died; like the missionary, they did not take the wind seriously enough. But the dogs are friends to the wind, and they will probably get back to the village. Sometimes dogs don't; they lie down and die. They know, when they stop, that the end has come. Dogs never stop 'for rest.' These dogs would see me, and I would be a wonderful time for them. They would be able to stop, but not die. Dead, I would give them life. My spirit would be in the sky, on a cloud, quiet and pleased; my body in the dogs, maybe part of their strong legs, maybe part of their strong voices. I have talked softer and softer lately. How good it would be if I could become a dog's bark or cry or howl — or its bite. When I see our dogs eat, I can't stop watching until they are done."

She is done herself, for a while. She moves back and forth: daydreams, some dozing, maybe "sleep-pictures," and then the talk that goes with wakefulness. She knows the word "dream," of course; she speaks English, as well as an Eskimo dialect. But she likes to think of those dreams as "pictures." There are, besides the "sleep-pictures," the ones she has while sitting or resting on her bed, or cooking; they are "day-pictures." Her husband is gone, but she thinks of him a lot, *sees* him. He was an expert hunter; he never missed a duck or goose or caribou with his gun. He could spot a seal and take aim and "get" it so quickly that others invoked spirits, sometimes, in explanation — the hand of Fate or God, striking at nature's sea life or animal life, in the interests of a particular expedition of Eskimos! She often went hunting with him. She was a restless one, when younger. And something of an iconoclast or maverick. She liked to cook and care for her six children, three boys, three girls, but she also liked to go hunting with the men, so long as they were headed inland, not for the sea. Sometimes she asked her mother to mind the children when "a good chance" came up. There was a time when she thought a man's "spirit" had come into her, by mistake, and was unable to depart. Once, when a young mother, she became terribly sick, could not hold down food, was afraid her days were limited indeed. She believed that a man's spirit was trying to break out from her. Had she not just returned from hunting? Had she not left young children for several days?

The vomiting eventually stopped. She had cut herself, let some blood flow: an Eskimo version of acupuncture — no rare gesture among her people. She remembers, in her old age, how it felt — to vomit, to bleed, to hover between this world and another, meanwhile seeing, more intensely than ever, various "day-pictures" and "sleep-pictures." As a matter of fact, like others her age elsewhere in the world, she remembers those past moments, experiences, tests, trials of a hard but satisfying and adventurous life, better than the details of her more recent life: "I can't remember much since my husband died. For a while I went to sleep sure that I would join him, and woke up surprised, *very* surprised, that I was still here in this house of ours, this house we built together. I would open my eyes and expect to be crossing the land, going toward the caribou. Instead, I would see the stove — that coffeepot of mine. I love it and hate it! I like the coffee, but I burn myself often. I am forgetful. When I was younger, my mother told me I was a bad girl, and I should stop being like a boy. I should stay *still*. Well, here I am, still! She must be smiling now. I see her smiling. I hear her chuckling. She had a soft laugh. She would be cutting fish or meat, and she would laugh. No reason, except her own. The missionary once asked her why she laughed so often to herself. She laughed again, and said she enjoyed her brother's stories. My uncle was with her, even when he was away hunting. They were always together. When he left us, my mother did too, a season later. I think I liked him more than I did my father.

"My father was the first one in our village to drink. I don't know why he did. The missionary said, often, that he knew why. But white people do a lot of talking, and they believe themselves, *always*. Often we don't believe them — but we listen. Oh, sometimes we *seem* to listen! Eskimos don't 'understand' as much as white people. I used to argue with the missionary, when he told me that he wanted to 'explain' his religion to my people. I would say that if he just let us come to his church, and ask us to pray, then we *would* believe. Why not? But the more he had those 'classes,' and the more he gave his 'talks,' and his 'sermons,' the more we became captured by him — and not real believers. But he meant us no harm. And he was against liquor.

"I have been against liquor all my life. A glass of wine is enough for anyone! I told my father he was treating himself like a ghost. He was *making* himself a ghost. The ghosts are the bad spirits. They wander all over. They have no home. I think they are mostly men. Men who drink! I may have had a man's spirit in me for a long while, but it wasn't a ghost! And finally, I was left alone; the spirit left me. I can remember the moment — and the many days that came before that moment. I felt the fists, hitting me in the belly. I felt the hands, pulling at my chest, trying to reach my mouth, so that they could get out. I tried to help. I didn't want my body to be a jail! I reached into my mouth with my own hands, hoping to touch the hands of the spirit. I vomited and vomited. But no luck — for days, no luck. That is why I cut myself. I sat down one day and remembered what my grandfather had told me. He said that if you let your blood run, you make yourself better. If there are spirits in you that want to go, they will leave with the blood. I had been counting on my stomach to do the work!

"After the blood began to run, I felt better. I let it run and run. I didn't touch the blood. I took the cup and left it outside, near our place where we keep caribou meat. It snowed that night. I threw up one more time. It was the worst time. My chest and stomach hurt so bad that I started crying. The missionary said I should cry when my husband left us, but that is the missionary's thinking: death. I told him I was happy for my husband. I expect to be with him soon. It is a man's right to go exploring first. A woman follows. If I had not cut myself, I would have left first — a long time ago. Either the man's spirit in me would go, or I would go. It was either the spirit would take me, or I would release the spirit! Once the spirit had left me, I was free to stay here. Afterward, I stopped going out hunting — well, most of the time. I wasn't as fast a runner. I walked slower. I used to walk so fast, when I was a girl, my mother told me I was being chased. I guess the spirit was pushing me! When the spirit left, I could slow down a lot. And here I am, so quiet that I wonder what my legs are thinking! No wonder they have become weak. No wonder they send me all those complaints — sighs and groans and cries. I hear the minister use those words — the sighs and groans and cries of Jesus Christ and His disciples. My feet have been my disciples, and I have not been as nice to them as I have been to strangers from the lower forty-eight!"

A faint smile. A twinkle of her wide-open eyes. A prolonged silence. She lifts her right arm, uses the hand to push back her hair, gray but not white. She wonders whether she will live to have all-white hair. Probably not. She remembers her grandmother's hair — remembers the pride of the old grandmother: not a touch of black. If only that would be the case with her! She is sure her "spirit" would be especially fond of an all-white head of hair. In her more fanciful moments, she dares specify where her "spirit" is — what its color is, and how it makes do, so to speak: "I woke up this morning and I thought of some geese. I saw them at night in my sleep. They were circling over this house. I think they wanted me to join them! They made so much noise. I waved at them, then I began to worry that they would wake everyone up, so I motioned to them that they should quiet down or fly away. They stayed, circling around and around. I got dizzy looking at them. I think I woke up for a few seconds, but I went right back to sleep, and there they were again. This time, one of the geese, all white, came close to me and I saw the eyes, and I was sure I was getting an invitation: come with us! I think my spirit was almost ready to fly away with the geese. Maybe it would have entered that white goose.

"But there are still some black hairs in my head! I'll be here a while longer. When my hair is all white, I'll surprise everyone; I'll fly away. I hope I don't get shot down! I told one of my grandchildren that my spirit would leave me and become a snowflake, or one of the geese or ducks, but today children laugh when I speak of an Eskimo's 'spirit.' They want proof! They want me to stop being 'old-fashioned.' They are like the missionary; they think the old Eskimos are 'superstitious.' Wait until that pipeline breaks, and there is oil all over Alaska, and the birds die and the caribou also die, and the children can't play without getting covered with kerosene or oil. Then they will wish they had flown away with me — gone way south with the geese! I tell them that, and they think I am being very funny. My oldest grandson said he wouldn't mind flying away on a plane, an air force bomber, but not with the geese! I am an old Eskimo, and he is a young one!"

More than anything else, she contrasts her view of the night, the winter darkness, with the response of young Eskimos to the same phenomenon. Her grandchildren are quick to seek light; she enjoys the shadows. A few years ago there was no electricity in the settlement; even so, the Eskimos survived the long winters, and certainly, she hastens to point out, never craved light simply to banish darkness. Now there is electricity, and at a gesture of the hand, an end to that darkness. But the old woman is not made especially happy by that achievement of modern science: "They put on the light; I close my eyes. I don't want to sit here under a bulb, when all over the land there is the darkness. I rest better in the dark. I have more adventures in my mind when there is nothing but me and the dark. I don't want to see the chairs or the stove too clearly. Sometimes I get too excited by the dark. Maybe it is madness; my daughter said one of the teachers told her that Eskimos become different people in the winter than they are in the summer — the madness of darkness.

"The summer is short, the winter is much longer. The winter is life; the summer is an interruption. The end of the winter is like the end of life; the Eskimo has become very tired, and the mind is playing tricks. My mind takes me into the corner of the room, or into the cracks of the floor. I once woke up, and I remembered being under the bearskin in one of the pictures that came to me while sleeping. I guess I was hiding from the light. I was afraid, under the skin, that if the light was put on (by one of my grandchildren) I would disappear, like the dark. Sometimes I think my spirit is counting my white hairs. Sometimes I think my spirit is resting in the darkness of my stomach. A time will come when the spirit will escape into the winter night — and then I will be an Eskimo looking for a place to live. Some of our people have not found a place. They live in the long winter night. They hide underground in the summer.

"I like to listen to the winter when the bulb is not burning with electricity. The snow is dark during the winter. The snow becomes light at the end of the winter. By then, it is time for the ground to appear, and the water. The stars tell us that darkness rules us. The stars are like a flame before the wind; they seem always ready to go out. They do. They disappear. Then they are lit up again. I do not understand what happens in the sky, why the weather changes. I mostly don't ask questions. I just stay here, and in the winter, doze and think. But there are moments when I am afraid of my own thoughts. They are like a strong wind. They are like snow, heavy snow, pulling things down, stopping everyone from moving — a blanket over our breathing.

"I once went wild. I was younger. The winter was one of the worst we've had. A lot of Eskimos died. I thought I was not getting enough air. I went outside. The air was so cold it froze my chest. I couldn't breathe. I fell to the ground. They took me inside. My eyes stopped working. I went into a deep sleep, my daughter told me later. I woke up tearing at my dress. I woke up choking. I woke up kicking. I went around and around the room. I thought I was one of our dogs, and I was circling, circling, and would soon stop and that would be my last action. I thought the darkness had taken me over, my body. I thought my eyes would pop out. I thought my eyes would become stars in the night. That's what the stars are, the eyes of the night. The night looks at us through the stars. The moon is the night's face. The moon laughs at our electric lamps. The moon smiles when we sit in the dark and talk to it. That's what I wanted to do when I woke up — go talk to the moon. I figured that if I could just talk to the moon, my head would clear. There was dark and fog in my head, and clouds and the sea's mist. For the only time in my life I wanted to go south, and never again come back to Alaska, and not be an Eskimo. I wanted to sit in the lower forty-eight someplace, and watch the sun shining. I had gone mad, they told me later."

She had been told by the minister and by a teacher and by an Eskimo who had spent time in Fairbanks — told and told and told — that there is a mind in each of us, and sometimes it doesn't work too well, or indeed, works badly, thereby prompting strange, puzzling, unsettling, weird, perverse, absurd thoughts and feelings. She had listened, looked off (by her own description) every time, wondered what sense a fox or a swan or a salmon would make of such talk, such observations or interpretations. It was getting warm when "they" all took the time to explain her actions to her — perhaps because, during the winter, they may have expected a recurrence, if not a relapse. Meanwhile she had not forgotten what had happened; rather, she had continued living her life — in the hope that, come warmer weather, she might have a chance to walk and walk, see the birds, spot the animals or fish, and talk with them. She had done so since childhood and found herself refreshed. She would do so every year until she left her body — and (who knows?) maybe even joined (for a while) one of those nonhuman creatures.

She is not very good at telling *how* that might happen — the transmigration of her soul, as a visitor might want to put it. She is not ready to affirm (to her grandchildren, never mind to a stranger) that such an event *will* happen, or even *can* happen. She merely wonders out loud whether there might not be a "spirit" in a person, and whether that "spirit" might not wander about the Arctic, and occasionally settle for a spell of residence within an animal, a bird, a fish. Let those who want to "study" her, figure her out, know her every thought, not to mention her "beliefs," "customs," "rituals," guess what she "really" banks on, or swears by. She herself smiles, looks off — her eyes reaching for a bird, moving with the bird's movements, leaving the bird reluctantly when it has escaped her field of vision. There is the madness of the darkness, she may well be thinking, and the madness of questions, definitions, conclusions, words and more words. So a stranger dares presume — after hearing the woman's grandson say that she once told him that birds are enviably able to move, to travel, to fly, to see so much and yet be quiet about all they have looked at and come to know: the routes, the pathways, the cycles of weather, the refuges or opportunities which the earth, the sun, the trees, the wind all offer.

2
Light's Coming

Guns have always meant a lot to him. As a boy he remembers wishing for a gun of his own, wondering when, when, when. He would say precisely those three words to his mother and father. He still does repeat certain words at certain times, including "when." He will be getting ready to go hunting, and he switches to an oddly impersonal line of inquiry: "When, when, when will the thaw end? This hunter wants to go out and catch food, not fight snow and mud. This Eskimo has had enough of the winter — enough, enough, enough!" The words on paper convey a more angry tone than the speaker reveals, or (a visitor realizes eventually) intends to reveal. The Eskimo wants to convey impatience, a touch of irritation, but not anger or outrage.

He is an Eskimo man of twenty-five, married and the father of three children, with a fourth on the way. He is short, a bit stocky, but fast with his legs, nimble with his hands. He has what seems to a visitor the patience of Job — and then some. He seems able to stand near a hole in the ice, holding a fishing line, for hours without moving at all. He will stare at the ice, or at the sky. He will think his thoughts: "I talk with the fish. I remind them that there are more of them than of us Eskimos! I ask them to stop and do me a favor — one of them, at least! Most of the time, though, I just look at the clouds, or the trees near the river. I hear my father talking; he's dead, but he's alive in me. His voice will live as long as I do. Maybe my voice will last through the lives of my children. That's long enough!

"My father used to talk to me about the Eskimo people. He told me that we are here because God decided he wanted to test people, really test them. The Eskimos are God's special children; the minister told my father that, and he told us that. He

116

wanted me to feel proud that I knew how to fish in the winter, and go hunting, and aim the gun. He told me it's just as important to stand here and wait for a fish as to pick up a gun and aim it and fire it. It's more fun to shoot. I like hunting. But I never get a chance to think when I hunt. When I fish, in the winter, I can think. I can sing to myself. I can listen to my father — and my grandfather. I can remember the best times I've had in my life — when I got married, when my sister did, when the children were born, when my father called me to him and told me he was proud of me."

That pride fills him up; he becomes silent, enjoys recalling the last-mentioned moment. He closes his eyes, so that he can see nothing except his father, himself. They had gone hunting; they had been surprised by a sudden storm; they had struggled home, bearing the felled ducks, one of which the youth had brought down. The father had told the son that he was a good shot, a loyal and conscientious son. Over and over again the son, now a father, evokes the scene in his mind, and awaits the moment when he will have something important, something unforgettable, to say to his own oldest son, then to the next oldest, and so on: the life of an Eskimo, the life of a father, the life of a hunter and provider, the life of a teacher. The moments he remembers are indeed awaiting repetition — as if they have a life of their own, as if they are spirits of sorts. So he says: "The time my father told me I was good with a rifle is inside me; it's a time I go back to, especially when I'm hunting or fishing. The children today watch television. I don't. I have my own television, inside me! And I'm in the picture, and so is my father! We used to hear a lot of talk when I was a boy about ghosts and spirits. The priest who came here talked about ghosts, and the Holy Ghost. My grandfather talked about spirits. He said that when something important happens, a spirit can be there, and the spirit takes over; the spirit keeps whispering into your ears, telling you things and reminding you of things. Sometimes I will be fishing or hunting, and the wind rises, and I know it's a spirit talking to me, and then I find myself going back to something that I did, or I heard, or I saw. Then the spirit goes away and I feel a tug of the line, or see a bird, a caribou, and shoot. No spirit wants to be there all the time, crowding you. The spirits like to come and go — just like darkness and light, the winter and the summer."

For him there are only those two seasons. He doesn't talk about spring or autumn. He refers to the end of the long darkness, and the beginning of the time when there is light and more light — and no end, it seems, to light. Once he talked about the stirrings within him when he realizes that "light is coming." He becomes "a different person." He wonders whether he will be able to maintain the rhythm of his life, fulfill his responsibilities. After all, the brief summer is itself part of the winter. One prepares, during a respite, for the long, arduous haul ahead. Yet the break in the winter prompts doubt, even a touch of fear. Will the mind break, too? And the light, the coming of the light, the apparent triumph, utter and lasting, of the light, prompts nervous questions — of a kind Western, existentialist philosophers ask rather often, perhaps unaware that others, far off and "uneducated," have similar inquiries in mind: "When the sun first shows itself to us, we ask each other if it's true that the day has come. I used to think there was a big fight in the sky, between the sun and the moon. The moon fights for the night; the sun has to win over the moon, and then the sky becomes light. My aunt told us stories like that. The schoolteachers don't agree. They know 'the facts.' My son always tells me about 'the facts.' But you can't measure everything with a ruler. When I see the clouds break wide open, and the light begins to shine on us, I'm convinced that the spirits loyal to the sun are dancing in the sky, and the spirits loyal to the moon are running for shelter. It is going to be hard for the night; by the middle of the summer, the darkness will be gone completely.

"It is 'all or nothing at all' here. When I was in the army I heard the song, and I thought of Alaska and my people and the darkness we have for many months, and the light we have for a few weeks. I would wonder why. Are we being tested by God? The priest tells us that, and the minister; they come here and try to tell us what to believe in — their God. We do; but we're Eskimos, and we have our own ideas. I wonder if there is a God for the white man, and another one for the Eskimo. Is there a God at all? I wonder sometimes. Is there a God of the night and a God of the day? My son told the teacher that he had heard me ask that question, and the teacher said there is only *one* God. That is the way the white visitors up here think; they mean to be our friends, but they think they know everything, and they think they have the duty to make sure we know what they know. I guess we do; but we know a few things they don't know."

He stops there; one thing he knows is not to enumerate too emphatically *his* ideas or certainties, as compared to those of others. He does not pretend to know for a fact what other Eskimos believe, or for that matter, what they (or he) ought to believe. He leaves pieties or rhetorical postures or "truth" to others — the teachers, ministers, priests who have come to his settlement, among others, over the decades. All he can do is be an Eskimo hunter and fisherman who happens to live by the demands of a harsh, challenging environment, and every once in a while relax enough to stop and think about the why's of existence. He himself explains that he ordinarily has no time for why's — and that he sometimes has almost too much time, not to mention a reason or two, for various ruminations: "The teachers taught us how to tell time, how to look at calendars. I forgot a long while ago what they said! We try to listen, but we don't always remember. My father told me how to aim a gun, and that is how we stay alive — through hunting and fishing. When I was in the army

I tried to tell some of my friends what our summers are like — light without nights. The men thought I was making a lot out of a little. That's what they told me. But they were not right.

"You have to live here to know what the summer can be like — especially when you've been through a long winter. I get dizzy sometimes in the summer. I feel myself ready to stumble. I've stood still, but the world seems to go around and around. Sometimes I close my eyes and try to keep them closed. But the light pulls on them, draws them open again. I love the light when it first comes. I am happy to see it go when the summer is ending. I am tired of the warm weather, and my eyes hurt from looking, day and night looking. My eyes want to leave the world and let me make my own pictures, not see people and dogs and the houses and the visitors who come through.

"I was told by a priest that I may have a sickness, because in the summer I have fainted. I have fallen down and dark comes upon me, and I don't know how long it has been, but I wake up as if I'd been through another winter, and the light was just beginning to shine on us. I find people looking at me, and I know I've fainted. It is my body's way of saying: enough! The light can be like alcohol. The light can make me see too much. I stop seeing real things. It is as if I am asleep, and having dreams, but I am wide awake. I met a doctor in the army, and I told him what happens, and he thought I was kidding him, or I was trying to get out of duty. But I wasn't. I don't know why the light goes to my head, but it does. They did tests in the army, and there was nothing wrong with me.

"The light is everywhere during July. It hits you in the face! I'll be standing near the river, and there is the light above, and the light coming at me from the water. I'll get drunk on the light! I'll throw myself at it — like a city Eskimo crawling, trying to find another can of beer. I'll try to stare at the sun — closer and closer to it, until I'm almost blind, and I have to look away. I can see the sun in the water, in the windows, in the flowers. The yellow flowers — small suns, making me blink. I want to stare, but I want to be rid of the light. I want to go back to the winter."

He has done so in dreams, in summer dreams. He has, upon occasion, gone to sleep, ever so briefly, in order, it seems, to touch base with darkness again. Then, more daytime, more activity, more light. He is no psychiatrist, but he knows the agitation of the summer, the curious, unreal, mental state that falls upon him and other Eskimos. And like a good clinician, he asks himself how long he will be able to keep pace with the rhythms of a special, brief, intense time of the year — and indeed, how it is possible that he can manage to be so "different" for so long: "I never seem to fall asleep and *stay* asleep. My mind is a wick in a lamp — lit up and burning, burning. I look at people, and I see the sun in their eyes. I feel the warmth of the sun in their voices. The sun can be a whip. In the winter I hurry the dogs with the leather strap. They don't mind; they are glad to be told to go faster, faster. In the summer the sun beats on us; it tells us that we must use up every second of time, never stop, except to change directions — keep moving, keep moving. The heat on my back, the heat in my face, is the sun's whip.

" 'I am tired of this summer,' my wife says every year. She wants to go to sleep and sleep and sleep. She wants to wake up and see the dark, the welcome dark. I had a dream a while back; the sun heated my thoughts and caused the dream. I was walking toward the ocean. I was in the middle of some grassland, following a path. The grass was high, so high I couldn't see the ocean; I only knew it was ahead. The grass was growing right before my eyes. At the start of the summer there is no grass; in a short while the grass becomes thick and tall. The grass was closing in on me. I thought I'd never get through it. I fell — a fox's hole. The fox ran away. I tried to shoot it, but my gun didn't go off. I felt useless.

"In hot weather I have no appetite. I don't like to eat at all. I drink water. I drink the Cokes my children like. I don't desire my wife. She is already wet from sweat. She doesn't want me to make her sweat more. In the dream I started sweating; I thought I would choke: the sun above, steady and hot; the grass, coming at me from all directions; the fox, laughing from a distance, daring me to chase, making fun of me for not being able to shoot; the air heavy on me, as if it was preventing me from breathing, rather than satisfying me; and the ocean — it seemed to be moving farther and farther away, like a radio that a child is carrying, and he moves down a path, and soon the noise is all gone. I aimed the gun at the sun. I pulled the trigger. I missed. I aimed again. I shot at the sky. I hit the sun! I heard glass breaking. The sun went out — like an electric bulb. It got dark right away. The grass pulled away from me. I could see the path, clear to the ocean. I could breathe again. The sweat went away. I felt my skin; it was dry. The fox stopped laughing at me and ran away. I was going to shoot it, but I decided to go to the ocean right away. I ran down the path and walked in, up to my knees. It was cool. It was dark — no light shining at me from the water. I decided to go fishing. I looked for my kayak, and then I woke up. I saw the light, and I was sad. I asked my wife if I'd made any noise during my sleep. She said yes, I had. I asked her if she knew what I'd been dreaming. She said yes. I asked her *what*. She said: 'Of the night.' I said yes."

For him, as for other Eskimos, the night is a familiar blanket, as reassuring as it is confining. The light is an abrupt, startling, confusing interlude — one that brings sights, sounds, smells, and one that gives the body a case of the jitters. He is relieved in the late summer, when the light rather suddenly begins to wane. He gets a little apprehensive in the late winter, when the light comes, stays, lingers longer and longer. Not that the light is an enemy; he knows all that it has to offer. He has heard his people's stories about the sun — its prolonged disappearance from the Arctic, its eventual, triumphant return. And each year he recalls what his grandfather used to tell him: "He said that once the sun was here all the time. It was warm in Alaska. But the stars and the moon wanted a place of their own. They asked the sun to leave, go down to the lower forty-eight. The sun said no. The sun laughed at the moon and the stars. But the wind joined up with them and drove the sun away. Snow came, and ice. It was dark for many years. Then the sun came back, a little. Each year the sun fights to stay. Each year the sun wins for a while — but then it loses. It would be bad if the sun gave up on us. We couldn't last without the sun. Soon the fish would die, and the caribou would die. We'd all die.

"My sons say the white people would help us. They would, I'm sure. They'd come with big planes and try to take us out. They might even get huge lamps — make a sun for each village of ours. But we would want to stay, even without their lamps; we would live and hunt and fish, until there was nothing left to hunt and fish, and then we would stay in our homes, in the dark, and wait for the end. Have you ever seen a dog draw all its feet together, while lying down, and let out a loud sigh, and go into a deep, deep sleep? That would be us — our last, long darkness, with no light to come. But we are lucky; the sun still wants to be our visitor, and each year we start the race from the first light to the last light. In the middle of the race, when there is *only* light, we are running, running and afraid we will fall on our faces, out of breath. Sometimes we do fall; sometimes we don't."

At times he sat and stared at the tundra, pictured himself walking across it, toward a lake. At times he sat inside, on a chair, near a table with coffee on it. He recalled his army days, his tour of duty in Korea, and especially the hard winter weather there. He has never been able to figure out why it is that the one harsh Korean winter has haunted him — and at the time seemed so difficult for him to survive. Alaska's cold and snow, he knows, can be much more severe. He had a recurring fear, in Korea, that his battalion would run out of food; that the terrible weather would prevent supplies from being flown in. What would his fellow soldiers have done? His apprehensions were of the kind some Eskimos have about the majority of Eskimos. What is happening to Eskimos, a handful of them wonder, when village after village is at the mercy of the Coca-Cola Company, the various manufacturers of potato chips, the frozen food industry, and the airplanes that come weekly to the various landing strips?

In his more mischievous and anxious dreams, he portrays a number of misfortunes, if not outright disasters, then wakes up to contemplate the reality of his life. Especially during the briefer rest periods of the "light season" he becomes prey, to a degree, to his somewhat alarmed state of mind: "I watch some birds, and the next thing I know, I'm dreaming of them. I had a dream a little while ago — very strange; in it there was a plane trying to land, with food and mail, but the landing strip was muddy, and the plane got stuck and crashed. There were a few birds circling over the plane, and I think I myself started flying toward them!

"When I was a boy I wished I could fly — like a bird. Then I wished I could fly a plane. In Korea I got to fly on planes a lot. I'm glad I know how to take care of myself. I'd hate to be an Eskimo who lived off a check from the state of Alaska. I will take nothing from the government. I was proud to go in the army. I was proud to be a soldier. I don't want money in return; and I don't want to sit here, all week, waiting for a plane to come. I'm glad the plane I saw in the dream got stuck! Birds never get stuck. In the army they told us never to worry; planes can get anywhere, except in the worst weather. But I have stumbled into two airplanes that have crashed — just in the land near our village. They say we're under the 'road' the pilots use when flying south from Fairbanks. I've never gone near the crashed planes. I just have stood there and looked. In the summer my children want to go exploring, look inside the planes, but I tell them no, to stay away. The white people are always searching for wrecks. They have come through here a lot, asking us if we've seen a plane that had to land. They think we spend our time keeping track of them and their planes and their boats and their lost people.

"Hunters from the lower forty-eight come here during the long days, looking for animals to kill. The hunters want furs; they bring so much food, they end up leaving it behind. They do not hunt in order to eat; they hunt in order to cut marks in their belts, and show off when they return home. I do not understand them; I never will. In the army I learned about them. They waste everything — food, water, clothes. They are always throwing something away; so much got called 'surplus.' I wondered why we were in Korea! The Koreans are good at taking care of themselves. They work hard, and they don't waste anything. They should go to America — to the lower forty-eight — and help take care of Americans! I am sure the Eskimos or the Koreans could help Americans to take better care of themselves. My son looks at the planes flying over us, and wonders if he'll ever get to be in one of them. I tell him I was in many, and it was more dangerous than being in a kayak when the ice is moving. There is always for us a chance to think fast, move fast; for the white people, when the engine stops working, that is the end!"

He becomes shy as he thinks about some of his wilder, more extravagant moments, when he has sat in front of his house and wondered whether the sun might not, one day, decide to banish the white man's engines — melt them. He knows that his mind's idle thoughts are absurd; if a machine goes that way, life would not be tolerable for any human being, himself included. Still, on especially warm days the heat goes to his head; and so do the mosquitoes and flies. He once saw a fellow soldier go crazy in Korea, and he has wondered whether those mosquitoes and flies won't, one day, drive him in that direction. When it gets so warm he is sweaty and all the more attractive (he believes) to various bugs, he becomes obsessed with them. They are "bad spirits." On their account he dreads the summer. He speaks not only for himself, but for his people as a whole, and even for the dogs of the Arctic: "They destroy our people, and our dogs; they make us shake with anger. Even the buzz of a mosquito makes me want to run in circles, shouting and firing my gun. Only mosquitoes on my skin make me want to get on a motorboat and ride and ride — until the light has begun to leave us, and it is cold, and they are all gone, the *pests*. I remember that word from the army: 'pest control.' I don't trust a lot of the ideas the white people have — their big machines and oil pipelines, the planes and helicopters they send all over Alaska. But if they could get rid of the mosquitoes with a machine, I'd be very happy."

The more he talks about the various bugs, the more he reveals the inclination he has to see them as part of a vivid moral drama, of sorts, that he has constructed in his mind — a means of explaining to himself some of the struggles that life inevitably causes. The mosquitoes, after all, are bothersome — and so must (as he sees it) be a part of a larger evil abroad the tundra he knows so well: "The dogs growl at the mosquitoes; it is in a dog's blood to know an enemy. I wonder if in mosquitoes there aren't the spirits of all the small and mean people of the world — the people who tell lies and cheat and suck the blood of their neighbors, and then die, and become mosquitoes. My grandmother said that when she killed a mosquito she was helping to clean our village. Flies and mosquitoes look for our weaknesses, and try to feed off them. When I have a cut, I find the bugs trying to land on the cut. They want my blood. They bring poison to us. The sun draws those bugs out of the earth and gives them life. They are kept going by the heat. When it gets cooler, they die. When it gets warmer, there are more and more of them. If we had hot weather here, we would be fighting for the air we breathe; we would be inhaling mosquitoes and swallowing mosquitoes, and we would get sick, and we would die. Then the mosquitoes and flies would stick to our bodies, the way we see happen when we shoot a fox. They are there as soon as the bullet hits the animal, and we have to keep chasing them away. It is dangerous, the season of light."

During the apparently endless days, light and more light, he finds himself sweating mentally as well as physically. When he sweats on his forehead, he stops, sits, pictures snow falling, the ice on the river thick and hard to break through, the wind cutting him to pieces. He feels a chill of memory; the sweat loses its hold on him.

But minutes later his head is warming up dangerously. He is at a loss: to start moving and once again feel himself awash in sweat, or stay still and find his thoughts jumping in various directions and making him uncomfortable, to say the least? One time he will gladly suffer the discomfort of perspiration — move as fast as he can, the better to forget his mental life; at other moments, he finds a place where he can, actually, surrender himself to that life. A favorite place is an old mud house on a slight grassy slope, overlooking the sea. He craves a breeze from the sea; he craves the clouds, a little protection from the sun's intense presence. He carries with him, often, a few rocks, or a piece of wood or two. Why? For idle play — something to throw? For company, in fact: "I was taught not to kick stones, not to hurt wood. When I was in the army I met guys who were always picking up stones and throwing them, or breaking branches in two. We don't do that. There isn't very much wood around, and there aren't too many rocks either. My father told me to be careful with the wood I find: treat it like a child. He told me to be the same way with rocks. If you aren't careful, the wind can come and hurt you. The grass will carry it right to you. I will stand here, and see the grass begin to bend, and I know it's headed for me. I am being told to be careful! If I am careful, I can enjoy the wind, not turn from it.

"I like to sit up here and think. If I'm going to get hotter and hotter, I might as well be away from my children, and near the stones and the wood. My mother told me that if you let the light get to you, then you can get sick, and your spirit might leave you, and it will go to a rock or some wood, and you won't have any more trouble with the summers. When I used to tell my mother that I wished the winter would never end, because the summer made me sweat too much and the mosquitoes would bite me a lot, she told me not to worry — that my spirit would escape, if things got too bad, and go live in a rock behind the house, or in some wood someplace, and then there would be no more trouble. But I'm still here, saying to myself how much I'd rather be fighting my way across the snow and ice with my dogs, than sitting here closing my eyes, and opening them, and trying to forget something, and having it come right back at me!"

He is, once in a while, interested in talking about what the light's coming does to his mind's activity. Disciplines like psychology and psychiatry mean nothing to him, but he can look into his mind, in a way altogether his own, and come up with a mixture of reflection and memory that conveys a particular Eskimo man's effort to figure out the meaning of his life. And it is the sun that gets that effort going, heats it up to a near boiling point: "I am afraid of the summer. I am afraid that I will melt, and become a large puddle of bad dreams and worries. When the winter is here, we are all together, and we eat, and we sleep, and we enjoy ourselves. I lie beside my wife a lot. The children sleep a lot. In school, the teachers have respect for the night and the cold winds, and don't say bad things about Eskimos. But when the light gets stronger and stronger, the teachers forget that the Eskimos can stay alive in weather the white people run from. All that our children begin to hear is what the Eskimo *can't* do, or *doesn't* do. We don't go to the lower forty-eight and brag about ourselves and tell the people there how bad they are.

"My eyes begin to fill up in the summer sometimes. I am *not* crying. I don't know what the matter is. I hear buzzing in my ears, too — the noise of mosquitoes, even though there aren't any near me. I notice my skin; it itches, and not only from bites. It is alive, my skin — too alive. I am afraid that the skin is going to pull itself away from me — as if the sun was skinning me, just like I skin a seal or a caribou. I sit on the top of the little place we built to store our fish and meat in the winter, and I talk to my skin. I tell it to stay with me a little longer. I don't want my spirit to leave just yet. We don't know where we go after we leave our bodies, but I think we meet other spirits first, and maybe they decide together! I've wondered sometimes if the sun bothers the spirits of our ancestors the way it bothers me. I saw my grandfather yesterday. I spoke to him. I had thought of him while sitting and looking at the ocean, and then he was there, walking toward me. He just appeared — out of the water. Maybe he was moving from a seal to a caribou! Spirits move, just as our people do! The sun makes us all want to move! My thoughts run from the house to the ocean, from here to Korea and back. I see a cloud, and I wonder whether I might someday live in a cloud. I see a duck, and I am sure it is cooler than I am. I don't want to shoot the duck. I want to fly up to the duck and go with it. The ducks are friendly with the sun; they fly toward it, but they stay cool. We get hot; so do our dogs. I've seen dogs go mad. They foam. They jump and howl. They bite other dogs. They show their teeth to me; I fire my gun, and either they back down, or I have to shoot to kill. Thunder in the sky — that is a spirit telling us that we had better watch out, or we'll be in trouble, too. I snap at my children. I begin to dislike myself a lot. I pinch my skin; I like the pain — it takes my mind off the sweat and the itching."

His mind becomes dazed, prey to "bad spirits," during midsummer. He is afraid he will be claimed by the sun. He is afraid he will be turned into a mosquito, or carried off — a part of the warm air that moves across the Arctic region in June and July. He sees mud, puddles, animal or human excreta, and dreads a possible demise: his spirit as a fly, or as mud, or as *merde*. The missionary priest has a point, the Eskimo man muses, when he talks about "dust to dust." Is that to be his fate — from the still-young body of an Eskimo man to the stench and rot and clammy miasma of midsummer? One moment he is ready to yield, another time he begins to assert his authority, flex his mental muscles. The Arctic may be a place of danger and mystery, but the Eskimo people have been around for a long time, and no insistent, probing, enervating, beating sun has yet to vanquish the distant ice floes, the snow that stretches for miles and miles toward the Pole — a reminder of what soon will be right at his front door, and a promise of a certain stability and predictability, which, however, he stops taking for granted occasionally during the short-lived summer.

Above all, when his mind begins to lose its usual hold on life, he craves a place to hide, a respite of darkness amid the light: "I want to go inside our little place, and keep myself there, like we keep dried meat and fish there. I feel like the salmon, hanging out to dry under the sun; I am afraid I will dry up. I am afraid I will lose my strength. The wind will carry me across the land, and I will never stay in one place long. Each time the wind comes, I will rise up and go around and around, and then I will touch ground, but not for long. Up and down, up and down — no life for an Eskimo to live!

"I sat on top of our hill a little while ago — near our small place, empty in summer, full of food in winter. My back leaned on the wood. I fell asleep. I dreamed: a team of dogs, pulling me on the sled — but no snow. I told them to stop. I could walk. But no, they wanted to help me escape. The more I told them to stop, the faster they went. I reached for my gun. Why not shoot them? A dog who disobeys is a dog who has joined the mosquitoes! I couldn't pull the trigger — not because I didn't try! The gun was jammed. I guess I was not meant to shoot! I threw the gun away. I sat there and let the dogs be my master. The dogs and the sun. My back was wet, so wet I decided to take off my shirt. I threw it away, too. I was as crazy as some soldiers got in Korea during the winter. In Korea I helped many soldiers get through the cold weather. I talked with them. I told them stories of my people. But on that sled, I was going crazy. I stared at the sun. I didn't blink. I didn't cover my eyes. I didn't look away. I was ready to go blind! I laughed and laughed at the sun. Then I saw it — the sun's smile! The sun was telling me that I had a chance, a fighting chance. I heard the message in my ears: escape. That's what the dogs were trying to do, I suddenly realized. We were going so fast that I knew the dogs would have to stop soon. They did.

"A cemetery was nearby. I got off the sled. The dogs fell on the ground. I wasn't sure they were breathing. I wanted to walk, but I was dizzy from the ride. I was still hot, too. I could feel the sweat dripping down my back, crawling down my forehead; I looked up at the sun: no smile anymore. I looked at the cemetery: there was snow there! I could barely see the crosses! I thought the snow would move — and it did. The next thing I knew I was surrounded by snow; only my head was uncovered. My head was like the crosses, my body was buried. But the sun was still out, and I knew it was still summer. I thought I was *really* crazy this time! Then I went further into the snow — and all of a sudden I was inside an igloo. The sun was fooled; the sun was off my back. I was happy and safe. I just sat there — until I woke up."

He has never seen an igloo, but all the time while in the army he was asked about igloos: how to make them, and how to live in them. He has often walked in a cemetery near his village and found himself talking with the "spirits" of his grandparents, who were quite reassuring and comforting to him when he was a boy. He is his own psychoanalyst; he interprets his dream readily, tersely: "I guess I wanted to find a place to rest. The sun cannot get you if you stay in an igloo. If you die, the sun cannot cause you any more pain. When I first woke up, I thought I'd died and been buried. But I realized I was only trying to get cooled off! What better way than to end up in an igloo? Or to be in a cemetery, down in the ground?"

The shadows he sees in the cemetery near his own home are, for him, a silent protest by the dead against the sun. The dead, too, fear the light. The heat generated by the sun surely must disturb graves, and as well, the "spirits," which often hold solemn enclaves (he believes) in cemeteries. He always cocks his ears carefully when coming near the small graveyard. And in summer he has, once in a while, talked with the various ancestors, given them reports on the village happenings. He is convinced that some of the dead stay in the cemetery all winter; perhaps they have a "meeting place" well below their graves. But they go away for the summer — far north where there is cooler, less distracting and upsetting weather. Well above the Arctic Circle the sun has its match in the still-polar weather.

When he is desperate — and awake — he also sends his mind, his fantasies, his "spirit" far north, a necessary relief from too much warmth, and yes, too much consciousness: "The worst thing about the light's coming — it is my thoughts; they get stirred, like the tundra when the caribou herds run across it. The earth flies; so do my thoughts. I imagine myself far, far away — where the winter never leaves the land. The priest says Eskimos don't pray enough and 'contemplate God' enough. Maybe the sun is our God; we 'contemplate' it. But we hide from it — so it must be the white man's God. We believe in the white man's God, but we believe in our own spirits. In winter, the Eskimo is sure of himself. Winter is our time; summer is the white man's time. The priest says we are wrong when we tell him the sun is a god up there in the sky. Maybe the sun is the devil the priest talks about! It's supposed to be very hot in Hell!"

That is enough theology for him. He is a fool, he freely acknowledges, when he talks about God, gods, the devil, the star, the star of Satan, the sun, even the ghosts and "spirits" of his people's oral tradition. The best thing to do, he believes most of the time, is to face up to the summer — a brief spell, after all, and so, in the long run of the year, something quite bearable, if unpleasant or troubling psychologically. Even at the height of the summer, even in the middle of an apparently endless season, even when light exposes everything, draws out all secrets, rankles dogs and gives Eskimo people a collective case of the nerves, there are shadows to be seen,

127

sought out, enjoyed. His house defies the sun with a shadow. The school does. The church does. The dogs do. *He* does. So long as there is a shadow there is hope. The Eskimo people were put on this earth to confront and even tame the winter darkness. Summer with its changed life is a mere moment in an Arctic continuity that goes back over countless generations to some moment Eskimos have no interest in describing exactly or rendering in a symbolic story. They do, however, know for sure that when the first Eskimos came to Alaska it was under cover of a winter night, and the sun was nowhere to be seen, for days and days and days.

3
Distances

The Arctic coastal plain is flat, sandy, blessed with a network of lakes. The water is shallow. Sandbars and islands run parallel to a substantial stretch of the shore. Inland, the tundra seems limitless. The eyes are stopped only by an occasional clump of hemlocks, a burst of caribou, fast moving and soon enough out of sight. At about six or seven, certain Eskimo children ask their parents or schoolteachers whether the tundra ever ends. They are told about rivers that have their origins in mountain streams, about valleys that cut their way through rugged, uneven terrain. But they smile in disbelief — most of those stories Eskimo boys and girls only gradually come to accept as "true," or as eminently suggestive as well as entertaining, intriguing. In the summer those children, and their parents, too, become preoccupied with what is near at hand: the thaw, which turns glacial gravels and permafrost into a lacework of turbid puddles; the wild flowers, in all sizes and colors; the profusion of grasses, thick and sometimes deep; the carpet of mosses and lichens, deep green or white or brown. But all of that, close by and for a while arresting, is no real match for the commanding presence of the sea, the tundra, the sky — the mystery of space, of distances.

An Eskimo youth, a young woman of fourteen who once spent half a year in Fairbanks, comments on the village life she lives, and the life she saw in the city, as well as the life she knows millions of her fellow American citizens take for granted: "I remember waking up in the house we had in Fairbanks; I went to the window, and I saw — another house. I bent my neck and looked up, and there was the sky, a small piece of it — the size of fish or meat we have in the middle of the winter, not fish or

129

meat we eat in the summer! Everywhere we went there were houses or stores. We kept looking at walls. I couldn't see beyond a street; there were always cars and buildings. The sky was not the same sky I knew. There was no ocean. At school there was a playground, but across the street there were stores. My mother said she felt a lot of the time as if she wasn't getting enough air inside her. My father ended up in the bars at night, drinking. He didn't see anything except the beer inside a bottle.

"One day he came home and said he wanted to go back to our village; he wanted to stand near the ocean and look at the water, not drown in beer. We left the next day. My uncle has been in Fairbanks for a long time, but my father couldn't stay, and I'm glad we're back here. As soon as we got home, my grandmother told me to go say hello to the ocean, and to the ponds, and to take a walk through the grass, and to watch for foxes and say hello to them. And not to forget the sky; she never does — she's always looking at the sky and watching the clouds, and she can tell if the weather will change by the way the clouds go across the sky. She won't tell me her secret. She says I'll learn it by looking long enough myself!"

She does that; she looks and looks. She looks closely at flowers nearby, the short stems, the heavy blossoms. She looks closely at the snow — soft and clumpy, or crusty, or shimmering in its subtle lines, currents, and crosscurrents. She gazes — a mix of attention directed outward and a meditative mood. She scans the horizon, or the flocks of ducks, geese, birds: whither and with what dispatch and how many? She stares fixedly — the movements of a dog, a fox, a bird hold her in apparent thralldom, as she herself seems to realize: "I can't take my eyes off a duck sometimes. I pick one, and I follow it, until it lets me go — by flying far enough away. Then I am free to go away myself: I'm back looking at the clouds, and trying to see if they are running or walking, and if they bring summer rain or just themselves, with the sun melting them every once in a while.

"If you look far enough away, you see the point where the sky and the land join; that is where I would like to go. My father says you can never get there, because there is *always* a point, far away, where the sky and the land join! Maybe that is why the caribou herds keep running all over; they are trying to find that place! They must be looking for something; otherwise, they would stay still more, or only move when they see us. But I've watched them when they haven't seen me, and they keep going, going. I'm sure they are looking for a home — and it must be at that place where the sky and the land touch each other; then there wouldn't be anyplace farther to go. As long as there is more land to see, and a sky to look at, the caribou decide to keep moving. They must get tired every once in a while. They must close their eyes and stop staring out at the land and the sky."

She constantly refers to vision, to the subtleties of sight; and in so doing, she indicates what obtains her interest — the vast landscape, part of which she stands on, part of which she stands under, and part of which, she knows, enables her and others to stay alive. That last, the sea, is nourishing to her, but mystifying, too. She runs to the sea when she is unhappy — only, at times, to run away, toward land, because she is not *quite* soothed, and maybe made troubled afresh. Her life is a matter of balancing horizons — that of the water, that of the land, that of the air. She has been told since she was a young girl that she would have to learn to do so. She was told through stories, whose moral or instructional implications were not missed by her and the other grandchildren who listened: "My grandmother used to tell us we must all come listen to her. So, we did. She would point to the ocean, and tell us we must never forget its seals and fish and whales — our food. She would point to the land, and tell us that we are, all the time, guests of the land. We walk on it, and sit on it, and run on it, and our houses are on it, and our food — the caribou — are also its guests. She would point to the sky, and remind us that the sky brings us water, and brings us air, and the light of the summer.

"She would tell us how our people have kept alive all these years: we haven't forgotten the sky and the land and the ocean. My grandmother bows to the ocean, and to the sky and to the land every morning. She doesn't like bowing to the cross in church; she says the church is too small, and the cross is too big. She asked the priest why we don't pray outside in the summer. He said a church is a place you go inside — to speak with God. My grandmother says God is in the ocean, and in the sky, and under the ground. We can never see Him, but He is there, way off in the distance. You should look, she said, very hard — because He'll know you're trying to see Him, and when you go to sleep and die He'll remember you were thinking of Him."

She remembers times when she thinks she may have elicited a preburial day response from Him. She has found herself taking walks, or simply standing on a slight turn upward of the land, when, all of a sudden, the world around her seems responsive to *her*. She does not, afterward, say that such *was* the case. She never moves from the tentative to the convinced. But she has felt herself in the presence of a watchful, heedful universe, and the result has been a touch of awe, a moment of perplexed acquiescence — as if she can't quite believe what she has seen or heard and found so significant. She makes, finally, no effort to "resolve" her mystical side and her practical side, her Eskimo side and her American-educated side. She simply recalls how it went for her: "I walked to the ocean because I felt sick. My mother sends us to the ocean when we get sick. I had a pain in my belly. The teachers tell you to have a Coke, or milk. My mother says to take a walk, and look at the water, and way off, the ice. I did. I forgot about the pain. I got lost — in the ice. I pictured myself riding on a moving pack of ice. The next thing I knew, the wind came up; I felt it right on my face, strong. I guess I was brought back to shore by the wind!

"When I look way out, across the water, I am sure there is somebody there who sees me. God? I don't know. Maybe my grandmother was wrong. Maybe no one is there! Sometimes I stare at the sky, and watch the clouds in the summer, and suddenly they all scatter, and the sun is staring back at me! I don't just look away. I lower my head, then I turn toward the ocean. Maybe the sun doesn't like me trying to figure out what the weather will be. The teacher says in the lower forty-eight they have machines to predict the weather. In the naval station they have those machines — down the coast. But the sun fools them, and the clouds.

"I'll be running, and I kick up some land. I keep running. I kick up more land. Then I fall — a hole in the ground. I always feel I've been punished. The teachers send you out of the classroom; my grandmother warns you with a story; the land decides to trick you and make you stumble. I can swear I see a shadow, way off in the distance, when I get up. I can swear there is a reason for my falling; my grandmother says there is a reason. The soil has been kicked by my feet. I'll get in trouble. I can feel the 'ouch' coming from the ground. I might stop and try to put everything back in its place, or I might run even faster. Either way, I'll catch it later; I'll usually stumble. Or I'll see darkness ahead — a black cloud so far off it seems to be coming out of the land, not down from the sky. Then it's time to turn around and go home."

When she is back home she turns around again, looks again. She has an intent, wandering, searching pair of eyes. She seems to be wondering whether someone, something, has been following her — spirits, ghosts, one of those saints the priest talks about, maybe God Almighty Himself. They are all off there, in the distance — so she believes. The world ends — or begins — a step or two outside of the settlement she belongs to, a rather finite and circumscribed collection of houses, with a small store and a small school. There is nothing, really, between her community and any others in Alaska — no roads or railroad tracks or even pathways to connect one group of people to another. She and her cousins and friends don't make reference to other places, even neighboring villages — meaning a place fifty miles or one hundred miles away. Life is directed at survival from day to day — though a plane once a week does bring in mail and provisions.

Children as well as old people (the latter remember a time when no plane came, and when it was successful hunting and fishing, or starvation) regard the settlement as a spot in a stretch of infinity, a lone star in a sky whose mysteries are very much beyond everyone's reach, though (as always) there are plenty of explanations and theories around. The teachers have their maps, with mileages; the priest, his Bible and conviction that God is, to say the least, immanent and transcendent both — not unmindful of anyone, anywhere. But the girl looks up or straight outward — and

132

feels removed in space (and, maybe, time) from just about everyone and everything. She also feels, has been taught to feel, vulnerable as well as self-reliant: "A strong wind, and we suffer. We have to be prepared to be alone all winter. The plane may not come for weeks and weeks. It is us against the sea and the sky and the land; they send snow and wind and the worst cold against us, and we have to be strong. When I was small I remember asking my mother why the weather got so bad. She said it just did. My grandmother said no, the weather came from someplace — and there was probably trouble there, and that's why we get trouble here. But she wasn't sure what kind of trouble. My grandfather said he knew — the fights our ancestors had with other people keep going on, and they cause the storms we get here."

She remembers as a younger child standing beside her grandfather. He held her hand tightly. He told her to stare out across the tundra, not to blink, not to look away. If she did so, bowed her head or closed her eyes for any noticeable length of time, he told her why it was important for her to stand fast — with her head, her eyes, as well as her body. There are spirits waiting, watching, or, alas, venting their spleens, way over "there" — across the frozen soil and across the ice-covered sea, or across the water temporarily unlocked from winter's bondage, or beyond the visible sky. There is only one way Eskimos have learned to endure; they know to face up to extreme danger, to face down nature's unpredictable assaults. If a child is going to become, one day, a sturdy, tough-minded, inventive, and persevering hunter or fisherman, or a mother who gives hope to children in the face of the fiercest, most unyielding storms, then there is no better way to learn than on the shore's edge when a strong gust comes up, or amid the grasses of the tundra when the clouds gather ominously and the temperature falls, falls, and the snow begins to come down with a thickness and speed — all of which indicates that the summer is over, the light will slowly go away, and (as some Eskimos believe) the distant horizon will disappear.

The young woman explains how that last phenomenon happens, and why: "During the summer we have been allowed to look far, far away. There is light all the time, and we can see over to the islands and beyond them, and way inland, past several ponds. And there are no clouds a lot of the time, and we see the entire sky and the sun. Then winter comes, and we get to see very little. There is nothing far away to see. We are lucky to be able to walk to a friend's house and get there in the dark — against the heavy snow. The sea gets covered, and so does the land, and so does the sky: ice, snow, and clouds. In the winter my grandfather used to tell me it's all right to close your eyes and not even try to look outside. The harder you try to see, the less you do see because your eyes begin to go blind with fear!"

That said, she closes her eyes for a moment — even though it is now midsummer. But they are soon enough open, and she is looking across the bay at her favorite sight, place, spot: a cone-shaped rock that juts out of the water — a resting place for sea gulls. Those gulls have always meant a lot to her, maybe too much, she says. Her mother once told her to stop paying so much attention to sea gulls. She obeyed — or seemed to. She became a more covert observer of them. She came to believe that she had in her a sea gull's temperament, if not "spirit." She has spent minutes watching them, perched on that rock, watch the world. She observes them observing the Arctic coast from the air. She envies them for the grace of their carriage while flying. But she especially pays attention to them when they land on the rock. Then, for her, they are kindred souls. Then, for her, the distance between that rock and the shore becomes inconsequential.

She has them meditating as she does — thinking about the various Arctic scenes and trying to make some sense of things: "I wonder if the sea gulls see me. I've tried moving, to see if they would move. But they know the difference between near and far! If they were on the shore, here, and saw me move, they would fly away. Even here, they keep an eye on you, and if you're not *too* near, they'll stay on their feet, but watch you all the time. It's got so that I know if I take *one* more step, they'll fly off. The teacher says I should figure out the exact distance and keep testing the gulls, and then I'd be a scientist, and I'd have my proof — so many yards, and the birds take off! But I don't want to know how many yards. I want to play games, I guess! I can see them playing games with me; and they always win.

"Once, a gull let me come closer than ever before. I couldn't believe it! I thought I'd be able to touch it. I thought it was in trouble — the wings didn't work. I kept moving, nearer and nearer. All of a sudden the gull took off. I can hear its wings going, right now, in my ears! I'll never forget the noise — like waves, hitting the rocks. The gull didn't fly away; it flew right over me, back and forth. I saw its eyes, and it saw mine! I think it was trying to figure out what kind of Eskimo I am! It kept circling me. I decided to walk. The gull followed me. I was sure it was trying to be friendly. Then it landed, way up the shore. I ran toward it, and it flew away, out toward the rock. I think I scared it when I ran.

"My father always tells me that the distance between us and an animal or a bird or a fish is very important. If you're going to catch something, you have to figure out how near you can come. You have to know how far the bullet will go, and how far the line will stretch. You can't chase a bird; you can creep up on it, but you have to be very slow and patient. When you run, you're wasting your time. I've chased sea gulls, but that's having fun with them. If I want to get close to them, I take a step, and count to ten, and then another. But I've never got as close to a sea gull as I did that one time. My grandmother says the gull might 'know' me. Maybe an Eskimo's spirit is in the gull!"

At other times she leaves the shore, walks inland, kneels down and admires the summer flowers — a poppy, some Arctic cotton. She especially likes to look at the land when the snow has first fallen, or when it has melted down, but not disappeared. She notices patterns, designs, lines and circles of white that cover the tundra. She likes to make her own lines and circles, too — sketches of sorts on the snow. Her ears are as sensitive as her eyes. She listens to the gulls, hears the wind working its way through shrubs, plants, man-made nets or lines. She walks up to the drying salmon in the late summer and smells the fish, touches the fish, steps back and watches a beam of sun on the pink-red of the fish. She moves back, savors the fish again, now from a small distance; she reminds herself how full her stomach is, how relatively empty it will be in midwinter, when severe and repeated storms can jeopardize even a carefully stocked supply of provisions. She sits and watches the sun, falling late at night over the ocean — the strange pink color against the distant ice floes, the uncanny mixture of light and dark. And in winter she notices the blue color of the air: enough light to take the edge off the blackness, but not enough to let the color of things really stand out.

In the summer she has stood transfixed, it seems, by the sight of a boat out in the ocean. She hopes the boat will move in closer, but knows it will not. It is on its way to a harbor farther up the coast. Yet, for some reason, it has stopped, is biding its time. She wonders why — wonders whether the Eskimos would be alive today were it not for boats like that, and the planes that fly overhead, and the canned goods she has come to accept as inevitable, as helpful indeed. She has put the question to her grandparents, and heard their answer: "My grandfather said that we were here long before the white people had their planes and ships. My grandmother took me to the fish she has stored. She took me to the skins, hanging. She showed me the meat. She said I am going to school, and that's my trouble! She's not against the Eskimos' going to school; she just wants us to remember that the teachers should come see us, and take lessons from us. They spend a lot of time making sure they're all right until the next plane lands. We don't have to worry about the next plane."

It is a distance from her house to the school. She goes back and forth, literally and spiritually. She admires the tough, independent, self-sufficient ways of her parents and grandparents, yet has not failed to notice that they have stoves, pots and pans, canned goods — and recently, a snowmobile. She remembers when that last phenomenon first arrived in her community. She was excited by the machine — the strong, assertive noise, the colors, the complicated machinery, and not least, the effortless speed. The dogs were jealous, she was convinced. *She* was jealous — such an immediate and gratifying capacity to overcome distance, "destroy the space." That is what she said one day about the snowmobile: "It gets you from here to anywhere in a few seconds. There's no space left; you just get inside, and the machine goes, and you sit there and watch the land go by, and there's nothing left between you and anyplace. You destroy the space."

She treasures that space, those distances she has come to find so much a part of her life. She has not stopped taking rides on the snowmobile; has not ceased enjoying herself, feeling the thrill one might expect a person of her age, especially, to acknowledge. But she can get out, after laughing, even shrieking with apparent joy, and look gratefully across the tundra, or out toward the sea. No matter how fast that snowmobile goes, and no matter how promptly she gets taken in it from this place to that one, there are still farther distances — to the point, she knows, that the immense, boundless Arctic is more than a match for those roaring, cocky motors that belong to those boastfully painted metal bodies.

4
Closeness

The Eskimo boy has seen the sky turn gray, then almost black. Where is the sun? It is still summer, even if late in the season. The river is nearby. He moves toward it, sees the fish, so many of them — all the village needs, it seems. Abruptly he turns around, holds out his hands, as if he needs to feel with them, for corroboration, what his eyes have just glimpsed: snow. He immediately heads for home. He stops once, though, gets down on his seven-year-old knees, makes a pattern or two on the thin layer of snow, collects some in a ball, throws it, gets up, quickens his pace — until he is opening the door, announcing his discovery. They know. They have seen. They knew before it happened, so to speak. The first snow in that Arctic settlement often is a summer snow — and a reminder that one had best quicken the tempo of preparation for later, heavier falls. The drying fish had best be taken in; the pelts, also. Clothes left casually outside belong on the floor of the house. The fish nets ought be brought closer to the house; the knives and the guns, also.

The boy and his two younger sisters are told why all that brisk activity by a doting but well-organized, quick-stepping, and, if necessary, scolding grandfather: "I must teach our young ones that when the weather sends us signals, we have to pay attention. It is kind of the summer to say a polite good-bye. The summer comes quickly, out of breath, anxious to expose herself to us! We are excited ourselves! We start leaving things all over. Who cares about tools, when there is the summer to greet and enjoy! Soon we are in a daze, like the people who drink beer or whiskey. You can become drunk on the sun. You can forget where you've put things. You leave your shirt near the snowmobile. You *laugh* at the snowmobile — such a foolish machine. What use can it possibly be? The sun is here, and is strong, and will stay here forever! My poor wife — she goes everywhere trying to pick things up and keep a record of where we have all put our clothes and guns and knives and lines. She knows what will happen in a few months. Even my daughter, all grown up and the mother of three children, will forget what she has learned all her life, and act as if the summer is not a brief visitor, but a permanent guest. So, when I talk to my grandchildren I make sure, sometimes, that their mother is nearby and hears me. I know she does because she smiles and says *yes* to the children."

He is, perhaps, a bit hard on his daughter, and his grandchildren. They don't have his lively step when it comes to taking seriously weather changes in the late summer, but they know what to expect, come the end of August, and they even know what to expect in early July, when the sun appears triumphant. His daughter has never forgotten, in that regard, the lessons she learned as a child. She is quick to connect what is happening in the sky with what is, or should be, happening on the ground — among members of her family and other families that belong to the village. Her mind has a notion of territoriality, accessibility, jeopardy, vulnerability, the limits of possibility — all abstractions for others, in the oft-mentioned lower forty-eight, but not for her utterly concrete, practical, and constantly alert, appraising mind: "I know our friends and our enemies. Our dogs are our greatest friends. The ice out there, beyond the shore, is our biggest enemy. The ice would like to cover the water all year, and move up the shore, and crush us! I am being unfair, maybe, to the ice — the missionary minister says. But my uncle was killed out there in his boat — so fast my husband didn't know what happened until it was too late. They were out in their boats, and only my husband came back. He told us what we already knew when we saw him coming in alone: a victory for the ice.

"When the summer comes, the ice pulls away from the shore, but it is not gone. We know what is happening; the ice is waiting, waiting. The ice is gathering itself together — and getting ready for another winter. We are relaxing and spreading ourselves all over; we start moving away from our houses — all over the land and farther and farther into the ocean. The ice says: 'Go ahead — come nearer and nearer to us, and even follow the water in between the packs, but don't think you've seen the end of us. We'll outlast the summer sun, and we'll be back in a few months. We'll claim all the water again. We'll move up the shore. You'll be covered with snow, and the snow will harden, and we'll be on top of it, on top of you — ice on your roofs and your doors and your windows. You will breathe, and we will be on your face. We are always waiting; wherever there is water, even a little of it, we are ready to take over.' "

She stops, a bit in awe of the power and authority of the ice — and surprised, perhaps, by her own description. She decides to pull back a bit, apologize. She did not mean to exaggerate, or give the ice more credit for evil or malice than it deserves. After all, there is the snow, and there is the cold air. And there is the wind — so pleasant in the warm weather, so fearsome in the winter. The wind, for her, is the most restless and active of nature's elements; and the most immediate and pressing in everyday life. During warm days a gentle breeze suggests expansiveness, the appropriateness of casual abandon. Why not venture forth here and there? Why not pretend that the world beckons — now and always? The young mother is quite conscious of such a frame of mind: "I encourage the children to go out and have adventures for themselves. They are inside *so* much — most of the year. Why not go outside and *stay* outside? They are a little afraid to wander far — the first day or so. They look up to me — as our dogs do: the head up, the eyes toward mine! I don't talk to them; I keep moving myself. The schoolteacher talks more than enough to children. From me, they need something different — a leader, I guess! I go outside, when the sun is getting stronger and staying with us longer, and I open my arms, and I ask the children to copy me. A white visitor, a hunter, once saw us and said he thought we were saying welcome!

"I race with the children. I set a goal, and we all run toward it — the edge of the pond. When the flowers come out, I take the children to them, and we sit down and look. I tell them what my mother told me, and my grandmother told her, that flowers are a gift of the sun — it heats the land and draws them out. It is so cold here, the land; when the sun warms everything up, there is a celebration: the grass and flowers. And we celebrate, too! I take food with me, and the children and I sit in the grass and eat; we can barely see our house. At first they ask me where it is, and will it go away! I tell them they are young, and they will learn that the houses stay — even when the wind of the winter tries to take them away."

Soon the children have forgotten their worries; all summer they live relaxed, inquisitive lives. They poke into the earth's holes, chase sea gulls, hike toward the pond, warily step into it, abruptly pull away, only to see some bugs that need chasing, or a dog who is only too anxious to play a game. In mid-July one sees and hears hide-and-seek going on — a group of Eskimo children claiming the settlement and the land adjoining it as theirs. And for children of six or seven and older, there are expeditions — to the sea, over the tundra, up along a river. Confined for months to a home, a classroom, the boys and girls are ready to move and move. Occasionally they begin to get a bit forceful, if not truculent: "When the children come back from a trip with their father, they let me know what their father has shot or caught from the river. But they have been doing some hunting, too. They saw a plane in the sky, and they aimed and fired! The plane was coming down, but they decided to let it go — so they waved it on! They met some people from the oil companies, and my son says he could have 'captured' them. I asked him why he didn't! He said he didn't want them here. We have our jail — a room next to the store, where we put someone who has smuggled liquor into the village. If we captured the oil people, they'd drink a lot, and we couldn't fit them all into one small room. My son tells me that!

"I wonder what it will be like here, in the summers, for my children. There is talk that they will extend the oil pipeline toward us, or bring oil tankers in up the coast. We had liquor in this village, and then we got rid of it, even beer. A few fathers smuggle it in. I am not an old one, but I know there are changes taking place. The Eskimos are getting money from the oil companies, and we have to meet and decide what to do with the money. The children have seen snowmobiles and motorboats and hi-fi, and they want them. Even in the villages to the south, where the white man's machines haven't come yet, it's only a few years before the changes will come, and the last Eskimos in Alaska without machines and motors will be going zoom, zoom across the land, or listening to bang, bang on the hi-fi. And television, it is coming; one village after another is getting it. We were late, and some don't have any sets — but it will happen: the winds from the lower forty-eight blowing hard, and bringing not snow or rain, but all of the white people's toys and tricks and ideas!"

She has skirted annoyance, if not suspicion and outright resentment. She pulls back, tries to remember "the good side" of recent developments. There is food in an emergency. A doctor comes in, to help with sickness, and in the case of children, through shots, to prevent it. The plane brings news from relatives far away. Children who are very sick get flown out, come back healthy. If the elderly want the same care, they also may be taken to a hospital in a city, though they say no, it is fine to stay, and leave their bodies when the bodies have had enough and are ready to stop working. And there are all sorts of opportunities — schools in distant places that welcome the Eskimo young, and cities where Eskimos have gone, settled, come to live comfortable lives indeed.

Why not leave, see the world, stay away for a while, bring back knowledge, a new awareness of the world? She asks the question in her own way, with that kind of favorable rhetorical intent, but she is not at all convinced. She knows of dangers that have also come with "progress." She is, actually, afraid of an ultimate danger: "I am worried that by the time I have grandchildren, our people won't be together anymore. We'll be scattered all over Alaska, and into the lower forty-eight. Once our people were together. We had our villages along the coast, or up some rivers, or on islands. Now we have relatives in the cities, and our older children are going to schools there, or even in the lower forty-eight. We can't keep track of our own, even in this village. I used to know who expected a letter when the plane came, and who was sending a letter. When my grandmother was my age, there were no letters coming in or going out. I'm afraid my children and grandchildren will follow the letters — end up living someplace else. Then there will be a few of us old ones living here, and all the younger ones far away. There will be a lot of mail coming in here, and not so much leaving!

"A long time ago, our people used to move a lot; but then they settled down. They built homes, and stayed in one place. They followed the fish and caribou, but they came back to their houses. I guess they stopped being a herd of Eskimos, moving and moving and moving! But now we're moving again! Soon, we won't be a people. We'll be Mr. Joseph and Mrs. Thomas and all the names we've got from the missionaries and the fur trappers and the gold-crazy, money-drunk explorers! We'll be citizens of the United States of America — that's what the people from the federal government call us when they come here and talk to us about our land. They say we're citizens, and we should think of all that the United States of America does for its citizens. My sister asked them *what*. They didn't like the question. They said we should look around us. That's the trouble; we *have* looked around us! Out there, in the middle of the ocean, they are digging for oil. Up the river, they are digging for oil. They come here and want to build a radio tower. If you go hunting, you run into their radar stations. Their planes fly over us. Their boats come by us. Their music won't let us sleep. Their potato chips and Coca-Cola are as bad as their alcohol. We have become their slaves.

"I used to hear my grandmother talk like that, and I thought she was getting tired, and was being unfair. I used to defend the white people from the lower forty-eight who come up here. The priest tries to help us. The doctor does his best; his medicine saved my younger brother's life, I know that for sure. The children of this village are learning a lot from the teachers; and some of them are very nice. One or two have tried to be like my grandparents — live the way our ancestors did. There is a teacher here who doesn't want electricity in his house. He built it himself, and he lives like an old Eskimo, not a white man from the lower forty-eight. He teaches our children what electricity is, but he won't live with it! We like him very much. So, it is hard to think of his people as enemies of ours. We don't want enemies. Even the winter is not an enemy. It can scare us; it can hurt us; it can even take our lives. But it does not feel a grudge toward us. It *is* — the winter. But white people, a lot of them, can't relax and try to live, and let other people alone. The white people, I am afraid to say, won't let people just stay as they are. They want us to go to church with them; they want us to teach them all we know about hunting and fishing, to be their guides; they want us to give them land we have, if there is something they want under it; they want us to help them build things, or go work for them in their cities.

And my father's uncle kept saying, until he died, that they want more than anything else for us to think like them! And they are getting their way — in everything, they are. That is true!"

She makes that last judgment with less bitterness than one might suppose. There is a fatalism to her appraisal of how life has gone and will go. She is not one (her people are not ones) to bear grudges, to let anger possess them. Occasional outbursts, yes — sometimes; but mostly there is her kind of wry and shrewd observation, and an astonishing resignation. It is as if, having learned to deal with the Arctic winters, the Eskimos are prepared for anything — the seductions of the summer interlude, the blandishments (and rapacious or merely bargaining presence) of the white people from the lower forty-eight. At times she even turns what she really believes to be an occasion for sadness into a not so gloomy acknowledgment of the fateful, the historically inevitable. Maybe it has been enough, to fight so long and hard against the Arctic weather. Maybe a people has just so long a life, even as individuals do. Has not the priest talked of the "lost tribes"? Do not the children learn that nations come and go — and entire civilizations? No philosopher, no historian, no anthropologist or ethnologist, she yet manages to take a "long view," and has what others might call a "cross-cultural perspective."

She even gets enough outside of herself to become a devil's advocate of sorts: "I don't think a small number of people can tell a large number of people what to do. There are *so* many of them — of white people. We are very few. We are not made to stand up and fight people. We are born to outwit the weather. We don't even fight the weather. The priest told us, when he first came, that we are soldiers, and we win a war every winter. But that is not so. He may be a 'soldier of Christ'; but we are here to talk with the wind and the snow and ice, and play games with them. My father told me a long time ago that when the first snow falls, I should taste some, and enjoy it. When the first bad storm comes, we should go outside for a few minutes and remind ourselves how many storms will follow, and how nice it will be, in the summer, when we are killing mosquitoes and complaining of sweat, and wishing we could sleep more, and wishing the sun would leave us for a while. Then it will be nice to remember the winter storms we had."

Those storms prompt her to think back. She remembers one time when the storm seemed endless, and the people almost ran out of food. She remembers one storm that lasted so long the village seemed buried to the outside world when the wind abated, the snow stopped, and an army plane flew over on a reconnoitering mission. She remembers a time when it became so cold they all thought they would freeze to death. The house, the stove — nothing could stop the seizure of cold: dozens and dozens of degrees below zero, no doubt. She describes what her family did then, what it does every winter, what (maybe) Eskimos will always have to do, if they are to stand a chance of continuing to be Eskimos — even if a new kind of Eskimo rather than the more traditional one: "I remember my mother; she always was asking us to come nearer and nearer. She told us that our only hope was closeness — to hold on to each other. If we got as close as we could, then we would keep each other as warm as was possible. We always come together in the winter. That is how Eskimos have lasted, year after year. Every time I start getting my children, at the end of the summer, to help collect everything left outside, I think of one really hard winter. We were in the house, and we were near the stove; but my mother said we had to be near each other, *really* near. We became one person! We were our one family, as close as could be — all of us with our arms and our feet joined. If we froze, we'd be one. If we died because we ran out of food, we'd be one.

"We sat there, and ate the last of our fish and meat. We had no food left. We decided not to move, just wait. But the wind stopped. The snow stopped. It became warmer. Our neighbors came; the dogs barked. We were alive, and we decided we would stay alive, at least until the next storm! I remember my mother making the decision that we should separate. I will hear her words until I die; and then maybe I will still hear her words, depending upon where my spirit goes: 'It is time for us to let go. We are going to be here a little longer, anyway.' I didn't want anyone to move. I said so. My father laughed. He said he agreed with me. He joked: the people would come, and they would bring us food and water, but we would stay as we are and tell stories and wait until we heard the first mosquito buzzing over us, coming toward our ears. Then we would all go running in different directions — and the mosquito would be confused: what happened to 'it,' us. After he spoke, we all laughed — and got up, and went in different directions!"

She tells in careful detail what each of them proceeded to do — as if she were talking of something that happened yesterday, not twenty years ago. Even confined to a log cabin, they had their respective rhythms of life — duties, interests, preoccupations. She and her brothers and sister began to play, tease, tumble over one another. Her mother tended the stove, melted snow. Her father talked with the visitors: how ought everyone in the village be helped — so that the supply of remaining food be made available to each person? But even then, help was forthcoming from the outside. Even then there were planes, of course, and a wireless set in a missionary's cabin, and soon enough: aid, first-aid, supplies, and not least, luxuries. The woman remembers one of the last — candy. And she remembers her mother's remarks — that she could not quite believe it, the presence of candy bars in the house, a day or two after the entire family had come together, the entangled roots of a certain tree, in an effort to face down, perhaps finally, a storm eventually known as one of Alaska's worst.

Candy — the grown woman keeps mentioning it. She still loves candy. She has long since taken it for granted — something the Eskimos of her village (and so many others) can now regard as a part of everyday life. She even, ironically, has come to associate candy bars with winter hardship, with the survival of her people. One winter, a rather mild one by Alaska's standards, she cast a glance at an old ice box, used as a storage bin. Inside were salt and sugar, bread and potato chips, Cokes and orange drink. A store had come to the settlement about a decade before, preceded by a naval outpost, whose purposes, to this day, the Eskimos don't really comprehend — or for that matter, care to. The store features Nestlé chocolate, and so does her home — a stack of bars that somehow seems to remain at a constant height. (A visitor discovers, through questions he considers suitably indirect and tactful, that there is another, hidden, supply, known only to the mother, who discreetly moves bars from one to the other stack. When the visitor learns that fact of a family's life, he also learns that his curiosity about the whole matter has been evident for some time, but his hosts have not wanted to embarrass him with answers to what they knew were his questions. So it goes: field work.)

The mother buys chocolate with a particular thought in mind; her children eat it as if it is a natural part of the Arctic world. The mother wonders whether there will be any "good" use of the chocolate she has faithfully stored, just in case the store, a half mile away, becomes an impossible journey during a storm: "I buy the chocolate with memories in my mind. My children eat it because of its taste. There is a difference! I wonder whether we're the last Eskimos to have any respect for the winter. I say respect, not fear. I was not brought up to be afraid of life here. The missionaries and teachers have always asked our people whether we are *afraid,* whether we *worry.* There is no point trying to answer them. Whatever you say, they come up with the answers they already knew before you started the talk! My father decided a long time ago that they are like that, our visitors, and I realize today how right he was.

"I don't mean harm, though, to any of our visitors. They have brought our people so much. Well, to be honest: so much good and so much bad. The chocolate, for instance — it tastes good, and if we had trouble here, and little food, the candy bars would be all the children would want or need; but their teeth begin to rot, like meat left under the hot sun. Anything that turns our people's teeth into rotten meat is not only a blessing! We have been eating meat for as long as we've been here, and fish, and some berries in the summer — and no rotten teeth. My mother says her grandmother used to say that we were all right here until the planes started landing in some of the villages. With the planes came liquor, and chocolate, and Cokes. The liquor turned our bodies into rotten flesh. The candy and Cokes turned our teeth rotten. What has the white man brought us? Who is he?

"My mother's grandmother asked those questions, and then people would sit in silence and wait for her answers. She told a story. She said that the sun was a friend of the Eskimos for a while, but then it tried to stay. The winter said no, I want to come back to my people; they know me and expect me. The sun said no, I want to stay where I am. I rule most other people, so why not the Eskimo? The winter said that no one in the world should have everything, not even the sun. The sun said that it would leave and never come back. The winter smiled and said nothing. The sun just stayed. The winter said, it would have to do something — and it did do something. It came to us with wind and cold and snow. The sun started leaving. But before it left it told the winter that it would be back — *and* that it would creep in, sneak in, during the winter, and fool it. The winter laughed: go ahead. But the sun is smart — and it did what it promised to do. Candy and Cokes are tricks of the sun! If we don't stay close in the winter, and keep our eyes on the candy and Coke, we'll all become rotten. We weren't made to sit and drink beer and chew gum and eat candy and have one Coke after another."

The woman is speaking for her great-grandmother, but also for herself. As she makes her statement, she realizes that there was more conviction to it years ago, when uttered by her ancestor. She realizes that the sun has taken hold, irretrievably. She realizes that there is, at best, a mere fighting chance that future Eskimos will be able to live through any part of the winter without chocolate and Coke, and their comrades of sorts: the pretzels and Popsicles, the potato chips and bubble gum — those strange names that have found their way above the Arctic Circle, such as Nehi and Red Dynamite and Nugget and Oh Henry! and Crunch. She realizes that all she can do is try to pass on to her children her memories and experiences — the stories she still cannot and does not want to forget. And try to make her peace with the new Eskimo life that is coming about. And even welcome some parts of that life. And wonder and worry and work — and live, stay alive, get through one moment and then the next, one season and then the next: the old Eskimo mandate. In the winters, especially during the severe storms that still come and for varying lengths of time evoke the past, the old Eskimo life, she has time to think about what she heard from her ancestors — in contrast to what her children hear in school, in church, in the store, near the landing strip. She is grateful for those memories, grateful to the winter and its perpetual harshness, grateful for the closeness, however passing.

THE ESKIMO
SNAPSHOTS

When visiting Eskimo families I have always shown my photographs, and on subsequent trips to the villages given many prints to the people I had met. Sometimes the Eskimos would bring out their own snapshots for me to see, or point out one or two tacked up in a special place on the wall.

They cherished particularly the oldest snapshots, some dating back more than fifty years. Often these old prints were so crumpled and torn that they seemed to have taken on a life of their own, beyond that of the subjects they portrayed.

From the start, their snapshots made a great impression on me, and I began to copy and collect them. At home, thousands of miles from Alaska, I would look over these photographs and compare them with my own.

Undoubtedly, when these snapshots were taken existence for the Eskimos was less complex than it is today. As an outsider, I knew I could never photograph the Eskimos the way they had photographed themselves. But I began to see that in my own photographs something was missing. I had been neglecting a joyful quality of the Eskimo people, a spirit so evident in their snapshots. Later, as I spent more time with the Eskimos, I came to photograph some of these joyful moments for myself.

The selection of snapshots that follows dates from the early 1930s to 1970, and tells of life in Eskimo villages on the southern Bering Sea coast of Alaska.

Alex Harris

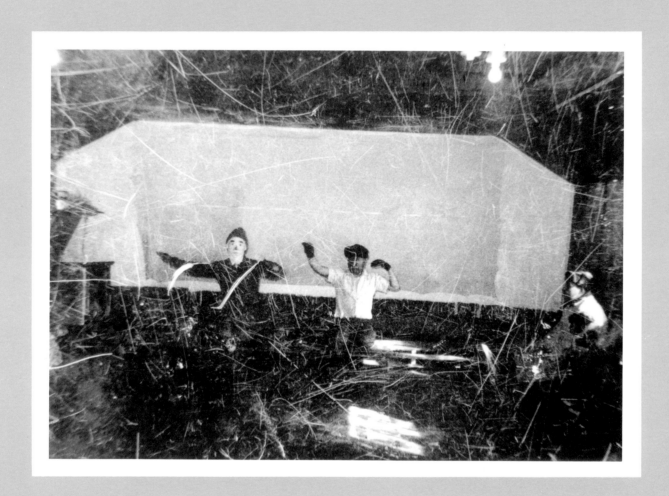

Type set in Optima by Vail-Ballou Press
Printed in duotone by Eastern Press
Paper supplied by S. D. Warren Paper Company
Bound by A. Horowitz and Son